"Anyone who has worked with children's catechesis knows the hurdles that prayer experiences must overcome to be more than preachy piety. The other danger is to make them all fun and games and to lose the sense of the sacred. Gwen Costello manages to avoid both pitfalls. I am warmed by her loving use of Scripture, and the real sense of reverence these services convey. She interweaves Mass responses and familiar prayers into the services with a naturalness that will help children sense the continuity of Catholic ritual. The children's participation is not incidental but integral to the prayer time. And the prayer goes somewhere in the action projects that conclude each service. Children are encouraged to see prayer as having an effect on those who do the praying, as well as on our world.

"Her method—to make the Advent season a time of sharing and not only the hope of getting; to make Lent a season of 'prayer, sacrifice, and service,' as she spins the familiar practices— is right on target. And her concern to keep the overhead low on the recommended materials will be deeply appreciated by teachers used to dipping into their own pockets to extend the religious education budget."

Alice Camille, M.Div., catechist
Author, *Exploring the Sunday Readings*

"I was pleased to receive Gwen Costello's book, *Classroom Prayer Services for the Days of Advent and Lent.* At the close of an academic year, it is refreshing to feast on a practical and well-informed resource for catechists.

"Often, our catechists have a great desire to include prayer experiences in their lessons but they feel limited by time and lack of creativity. This book will serve them very well, for it offers rich texts, prayerful reflections and actions, and a wide variety of contexts for prayer. A great gift for catechists that will certainly be used for many seasons to come."

Kathleen Flannery, OSU
Pastoral Associate
Holy Cross Church
Euclid, OH

"In this book, Gwen Costello has provided an invaluable spiritual resource for teachers, catechists, parents and, of course, children. These prayer services will help children ritualize practically every facet of Christian living. They effectively utilize the basic tenets of ritual: Scripture, symbol, silence, story, repetition, and the inclusion of guided meditation is an added bonus. In addition, they furnish opportunities for children to live their prayer beyond the service itself."

Sandra DeGidio, OSM
Author, *Sacraments Alive* and
Prayer Services for the Elderly

"These *Classroom Prayer Services for the Days of Advent and Lent* by Gwen Costello are a useful and practical resource for religious educators. Costello's simple and clear texts (more than 60 prayer services) integrate scripture, response, and activity well. The prayer experiences collected here truly present prayer as Costello's introduction promises: as 'total body-mind-heart response.' The activities and short games (like 'Bible Detective', p. 72) assure that an active role will be taken by the children for whom these prayer services are designed. While involvement is key, it is to Costello's credit that silence and listening are emphasized too—and modeled well. The variety of Advent and lenten themes which this text offers assure wide possibilities for its use."

Pamela Smith, SSCM
Director of Lay Ministry Programs
SS. Cyril and Methodius Seminary
Orchard Lake, MI

"*Classroom Prayer Services* is a welcome addition to the library of any pastor, DRE, or religion teacher. The prayer services are clearly outlined, including needed supplies. Each service is simple enough for the youngsters to participate in the prayers and activities. At the same time, the prayers and responses help to introduce more 'adult' prayer forms, all comfortably within our Catholic tradition. Opportunities for growth in public and private prayer abound."

Rev. Laurin J. Wenig
Author, *40 Days of Grace* and *In Joyful Expectation*
Pastor of 3 rural parishes, Archdiocese of Milwaukee

"*Classroom Prayer Services for the Days of Advent and Lent* will be a real help to catechists and teachers who want to provide prayerful experiences for their students. But more important, each service provides an opportunity for children to participate—not only in the prayer service itself, but actively as they carry out the message of their prayer. Gwen's book gives us fresh and abundant variety during Advent and Lent as we strive to keep our students involved and prayerful."

Marianne Slattery
Director of Religious Education
St. Noel Church
Willoughby Hills, OH

Classroom Prayer Services

for the Days of Advent and Lent

G W E N   C O S T E L L O

XXIII

TWENTY-THIRD PUBLICATIONS

Mystic, CT 06355

Twenty-Third Publications
185 Willow Street
P.O. Box 180
Mystic, CT 06355
(860) 536-2611
800-321-0411

ISBN 0-89622-737-5
Library of Congress Catalog Card Number 97-60728
Printed in the U.S.A.

Cover and interior illustrations were done by Holly Bewlay.

Dedication

With deep gratitude
I dedicate this book
to the thousands of
catechists, teachers, and DREs
who year after year
continue to proclaim
and share their faith
with the children and teenagers
in their parishes.

May God bless and reward you
abundantly.

Contents

Introduction   1

Part One: The Season of Advent

1.   Listening to God   4

2.   Give Us Advent Hearts   6

3.   Making Advent Choices   8

4.   Following Jesus   10

5.   Waiting with Mary   11

6.   Showing Respect   14

7.   Offering Kindness   16

8.   Spreading Good Cheer   18

9.   Waiting with the Saints   20

10. Proclaiming Our Faith   22

11. Listening to God   24

12. Counting Our Blessings   26

13. Come Lord Jesus   28

14. Recognizing Jesus   30

15. Learning to Love   31

16. Jesus Is among Us   33

17. Spreading Peace   35

18. Showing Our Thanks   37

19. Showing Our Joy   39

20. Learning Patience   41

21. Saying Thanks   43

22. Preparing for Christmas   45

23. Offering Our Gifts   47

Part Two: The Season of Lent

1.	We Prepare for Lent	50
2.	Keeping Close to God	52
3.	Learning to Pray	54
4.	Needing God	56
5.	Looking for Jesus	58
6.	Offering Peace	60
7.	God Always Forgives	61
8.	Going Forward with Jesus	63
9.	Loving One Another	65
10.	Healing Our Hurts	67
11.	Praying Always	69
12.	Listening to Jesus	71
13.	Sharing Our Light	73
14.	Living the Gospel	75
15.	Learning to Be Gentle	77
16.	Walking with Jesus	79
17.	Carrying Our Crosses	81
18.	Forgiving One Another	83
19.	Sharing Living Water	85
20.	Doing God's Will	87
21.	Making Others Happy	89
22.	Doing the Right Thing	91
23.	Loving Our Enemies	93
24.	Learning to Give "Alms"	95
25.	Healing Our Blindness	97
26.	Serving Others First	99

27.   Learning to Say No   101

28.   Turning the Other Cheek   103

29.   Coming from the Tomb   105

30.   Remembering Jesus   107

31.   Singing Hosanna   109

32.   Asking for Forgiveness   111

33.   Following Jesus   113

34.   Waiting for Easter   115

35.   Sharing Easter Joy   117

36.   Receiving the Holy Spirit   119

37.   Living in the Spirit   121

38.   Walking with the Spirit   123

Appendix One
   Prayers and Phrases   126

Appendix Two
   Guidelines for Guided Meditation   128

Appendix Three
   Get-Acquainted Activities   130

Classroom Prayer Services

Introduction

Prayer is essential to our relationship with God, but it is more than words. It is a total body-mind-heart response that involves silence, rituals, and repetition. This variety is important for us adults but even more important for children. They need to be as fully involved as possible in our class prayer experiences. Some of the ways you can involve them in celebrating God's presence are through processions, veneration of the Bible, prayer patterns (like litanies and repeated refrains), speaking parts, and blessings. The services in this book offer you opportunities to include many of these elements in your class prayer.

These services are intended to be used by teachers, catechists, and parents. They cover the liturgical seasons of Advent, Christmas, Lent, Easter, and Pentecost. All who gather with children, ages seven to twelve, on a regular basis can use these services. They can be used as part of a meeting, a class, a sacrament practice session, or a family meal. They can also be used as part of an Advent or Lent family workshop. They can be done in church, in classrooms, in meeting rooms, and in homes. In some cases, slight adaptations will have to be made to adjust to the environment. For example, if a given service is done in a home, the "prayer table" might actually be a dining room or kitchen table.

When possible and appropriate, I have used words or phrases from the Mass, the Bible, and traditional prayers in these services. I hope that this will help children make "connections" between liturgy, the Bible, and life, and to become familiar enough with biblical and liturgical words and phrases to use them often in their prayer. I have also included Catholic customs like praying to Mary and the saints, practicing virtue, fasting, and abstinence.

The following are some general guidelines that apply to all the services in this book.

1. Designate one place in your teaching area as the prayer table. This can be a desk, a small stand, or a portable table. Gather around this table for your class prayer services.

2. Always have a Bible on your prayer table during class prayer. You can either have it already on the table or have a child carry it to the table at the time of prayer. Children can take turns carrying the Bible, which they should always carry carefully and respectfully. Within each service the text from which the reading is drawn is cited, in case you want to have it read directly from the Bible. In almost all cases, the readings for these services are paraphrased for ease of understanding.

3. Always have a candle on your prayer table. A votive candle works best because there is less danger of spilling wax or tipping it over. Before you begin your class prayer, have a child light the candle. Again, allow children to take turns being the candle lighter.

4. Always practice with "readers" beforehand.

5. Also practice the refrains recited by "All" with the entire group beforehand.

6. If the children in your class are not used to silent prayer or guided meditation, see the guidelines in Appendix Two in the back of this book.

7. If they are not used to processions, you may want to practice before your actual prayer time. During processions there should as a rule be no talking (other than saying or chanting prayers and/or singing).

8. In groups where the children come from different schools or neighborhoods and do not know one another well, it can be very beneficial to do a get-acquainted or "icebreaking" activity with them before you invite them to pray together. It's also important, however, even for children who do know one another because it helps them relax and relate to one another in a lighthearted way before sharing prayer. See Appendix Three for suggestions.

9. One final note: Permission is granted to duplicate these services for the children in classes or groups who participate in them.

Part One: The Season of Advent

Christmas celebrates the Incarnation, the great mystery of God entering our world and dwelling among us. It is more than the birthday of the person named Jesus of Nazareth; indeed we don't know his historical birth date. Christmas is the birthday of God among us, for it offers all of us new life in Jesus—including the children we teach. Jesus the Christ is our Emmanuel, God with us.

Advent is a time of anticipation and preparation for the birth of Jesus. It is a time for Christians to think about what they can share with others in return for all the gifts God has given them, especially the gift of Jesus. Our culture offers a different message, however. It says: think about all the things you want, make lists, and make demands. There is no place for the babe born in Bethlehem in this scenario. There is only place for our greedy selves.

We have to make a special effort with our children during Advent to direct them away from selfish receiving to unselfish giving. Most of them *need* very little, but many in our world are in great need. Thus these services guide children toward sharing, caring, and giving as well as toward communication with God. Each focuses on a particular aspect of preparing for Christmas as followers of Christ in this day and age.

1. Listening to God

Introduction

Talk to children about silence. When, if ever, do they have moments of silence? How does it make them feel? Explain that all of us are uncomfortable to some extent with silence because we are so used to noise. Yet we need silence in our prayer that we might hear God speaking to us. Jesus is our guide in this. When he wanted to pray, he sought quiet places. Suggest to children that they practice being silent whenever they pray during Advent.

To Prepare

Have paper and pencils or pens available for each child. Gather around your prayer table on which is placed a lighted votive candle and a Bible (open to Matthew 14:22–23).

Leader	Loving God, teach us to pray. Teach us to be silent that we might hear your answer to our prayers. Help us today to practice listening to you in stillness and peace. Help us now to hear your Word and live it.
Reader One	In St. Matthew's Gospel it is clear that Jesus liked to be in a quiet place for his prayer. It is written: "Jesus went up the hillside quite alone, to pray."
Reader Two	Jesus, help us to be silent when others are speaking to us or teaching us, that we might hear your message through them.
All	May we always listen for your voice, dear God.
Reader Three	Help us to be silent, Jesus, when we are tempted to say unkind things about others or to hurt someone in any way with our words.
All	May we always listen for your guidance, dear God.
Leader	Jesus, our savior, we need your help to learn how to listen this Advent. We are so used to noise that silence seems strange. May we now listen silently to you in our prayer.
	Pause for a moment of silent prayer.
Leader	You speak to us often, God, our God, if only we would listen. Teach us how to pray in silence this Advent and always. We ask this…
All	In the name of the Father and of the Son and of the Holy Spirit. Amen.
Advent Action	Spend a few moments in each of your Advent classes praying in silence. Encourage children to close their eyes and bow their heads and to simply wait and listen. Lead the way by practicing silent prayer with them. Follow

this by inviting children to write a prayer thanking God for speaking to them. Encourage them to keep this prayer and say it throughout Advent.

Optional Activity

Have available supplies for making a class Advent wreath. You will need evergreens, four candles (three purple and one pink) a circular shape (styrofoam, wire, or a purchased Advent wreath), a ribbon for each candle (again three purple and one pink), and a tray or heavy piece of cardboard on which to place the wreath.

If your resources are limited, simply draw a large wreath with four candles surrounding it. Throughout Advent, when you gather for class prayer, place your Advent wreath on the prayer table in place of a votive candle. In the first week of Advent, light one candle; in the second week, two; in the third week three; and in the fourth week four. (If you are using a drawing, color in the flames on the various weeks.)

Before you use your class wreath for the first time, have this simple blessing ceremony.

Leader

We ask you, God, our creator, to bless this Advent wreath. May it remind us that Jesus is in our midst and that we are surrounded by his love and care.

Child One

Bless these candles on our wreath. May they remind us that Jesus is the Light of the World.

Child Two

Bless these evergreens on our wreath. May they remind us that Jesus' love for us is everlasting and that nothing we do will ever take it away.

Leader

May this wreath remind us to prepare well for Christmas, each and every day of the Advent season. We ask these things in Jesus' name.

All

Amen.

2. Give Us Advent Hearts

Introduction

Advent is a time of anticipation and preparation for the birth of Jesus. It is a time for Christians to reflect upon what they can share with others in return for all the gifts God has given them, especially the gift of Jesus. This service reminds children of the reason for the season.

To Prepare

On your prayer table, place a Bible (open to Matthew 25:34–40) and a candle (or your Advent wreath). For the activity, you will need old Christmas cards, construction paper, glue, and scissors.

Leader	Jesus, we want to prepare our hearts and minds to celebrate your birthday at Christmas. We want to think of things we can give you. Christmas is your birthday and we want to prepare presents for you. Help us to forget about ourselves for a while and to think only of you and how we can offer you love and joy.
All	May we offer you only love and joy this Advent.
Reader One	Help us, Jesus, to think more about you than about the presents we will get. Help us to think about the real meaning of Christmas.
Reader Two	We exchange gifts with one another as a way of celebrating Jesus' birthday. Yet what gifts can we give Jesus himself?
Leader	We can't give Jesus gifts directly. But remember what he says in the Bible: What you do to others, you do to me. That's why we give gifts to one another. It's a way of expressing our love for Jesus. Listen now to God's Word.
Reader Three	A reading from the Gospel of Matthew: Then he will say to those on his right, I was hungry and you gave me food; I was thirsty and you gave me drink; I was a stranger and you welcomed me. …As often as you did these things for my little ones, you did them for me. *The Gospel of the Lord.*
All	Praise to you, Lord Jesus Christ.
Leader	God is letting us know through these words that we are called to share our gifts with people who need them, not just with our family and friends. Then we will truly be giving a gift to Jesus.

Sharing is difficult and it means that we will have to think about the needs of others and put our own wants aside. Let's pray about this now. Close your eyes and answer these questions silently.

Pause briefly after each of these questions.

• Would you be willing to buy a gift for someone in need, for someone you don't even know?
• Would you be willing to spend some of your own money for such a gift?
• Do you ever think about Jesus as you prepare for Christmas?
• Do you talk to Jesus every day?
• Do you ask him to help you to think of others?

Picture Jesus now standing before you. Take a few minutes to talk to him about these things.

Allow two minutes or so for this.

Leader   Jesus, teach us how to think about you this Advent. Teach us to reach out to others, to the poor, the lonely, the sick, and the hungry. When we give gifts to them, we are giving gifts to you. Help us to be generous. Help us to be strong. We ask these things in the name of the Father, and of the Son, and of the Holy Spirit.

All   Amen.

Advent Action   Explain to the children that one small way they can begin to think of others this Advent is by making a card for someone who is lonely. Distribute the cards, glue, scissors, and construction paper. Encourage them to write their own messages on their finished cards, offering the person their love and prayers. Before they leave, remind them to actually give the card to someone who is lonely or sad.

3. Making Advent Choices

Introduction

Explain to children that during Advent it is good to balance the needs of others with our own. This means making choices that involve the good of others and not just our own. Encourage children to practice self-control during Advent (which strengthens their ability to make unselfish choices) in the ways described in this service.

To Prepare

Have pencils and small slips of paper available for each child. Gather around your prayer table on which are placed a lighted candle (or your Advent wreath) and a Bible (open to Ephesians 5:2). Also place there a container (a basket or bowl).

Leader	May we live our lives in love as Christ Jesus did. May all our choices be for the good of others rather than for our own good alone. Let us listen carefully now to this message from God's Word.
Reader One	In his letter to the Christians in Ephesus, St. Paul wrote: "Live your lives in love—the same sort of love Christ showed when he gave himself up for us in sacrifice to God."
Reader Two	Jesus, our brother, when we are angry, when we feel tired, when we are grouchy or in a bad mood, help us to practice self-control, here in religion class, at home, and at school.
All	Help us to make unselfish choices, Jesus, this Advent and always.
Reader Three	Jesus, our savior, when we are tempted to do the wrong thing, to steal, to lie, to cheat, or to speak unkindly of others, help us to choose the right thing.
All	Help us to make unselfish choices, Jesus, this Advent and always.
Leader	Making the right choice is not easy. We all sometimes forget to think of others and for this we ask God's pardon. Let us now talk to God in silence about our need for self-control.
	Pause for a moment of silent prayer.
Leader	Strengthen us, Jesus our brother and savior, that we might follow you in everything we do this day and throughout Advent.
All	Amen.

Advent Action   Suggest to children several ways that they can practice self-control at home, for example: letting others speak first; sharing a toy when they don't feel like it; saying please and thank you to parents; not running in the house; saying no to unhealthy habits like eating too many sweets; trying to eat a balanced diet that includes fruits and vegetables, etc.

Have them write this practice on one of the slips of paper and place these in a container on your prayer table. In subsequent Advent classes, remind children to be faithful to their practice.

Optional Activity   Write out on 3"x3" pieces of purple paper (one for each child), various choices children might make during Advent. Some should be "good" (Advent) choices, for example: offering the last cookie to someone else, visiting an elderly neighbor, letting someone get in line ahead of you, playing a game with a younger sister or brother. Some of the choices should be "bad" (selfish) choices, for example: hitting your sister or brother, lying about breaking a dish, talking back to a teacher, grabbing the last cookie.

Have children take turns drawing a card and then pantomiming the situation on it. Once the action is guessed, ask children to identify it as a good choice or a selfish one. Continue until each child has had a turn.

4. Following Jesus

Introduction

Explain to children that all of us need to be in touch with who we really are and how we need God's help. Advent is a special time in the church year for seeing ourselves clearly, talents as well as weaknesses. Encourage children to practice honesty in all that they do during Advent, with Jesus as their example.

To Prepare

Have cards prepared for each child (as below) as well as coloring supplies. Gather around your prayer table on which are placed a lighted candle and a Bible (open to John 14:6).

Leader	God, our Father, thank you for sending Jesus to guide and teach us. Help us, please, to follow him carefully, not just during Advent but always, so that we may know the way to you, the truth about ourselves, and how to share the life you offer. Open our minds as we listen now to your Word.
Reader One	Jesus said to his followers, "I am the way, and the truth, and the life."
All	May we follow you, Jesus; show us the way.
Reader Two	Help us to be honest with others this Advent, Holy Spirit, with our family members, with our teachers and classmates, and with everyone we meet.
All	May we follow you, Jesus; you teach us the truth.
Reader Three	May we be honest with you today, Jesus, our savior, by doing our best in this religion class with the gifts and talents we have received.
All	May we follow you, Jesus; you give us the gift of life.
Leader	God, our loving Father, show us the way to Jesus. Open our minds and hearts now to hear what he wants to say to us.
	Pause for a moment of silent prayer.
Leader	Jesus, please be our way, our truth, and our life, this Advent and always. We ask this…
All	…in the name of the Father, and of the Son, and of the Holy Spirit. Amen.
Advent Action	Give each child a card on which these words are written: "Jesus, show us the way, teach us the truth, and give us God's life." Have them decorate these and take them home as a reminder that Jesus is with them always.

5. Waiting with Mary

Introduction

Use this service throughout the four weeks of Advent. You might want to combine it with the blessing of and prayers around your class Advent wreath. Encourage children to pray to Mary often as they await the birth of Jesus at Christmas.

To Prepare

Place on your prayer table a Bible (open to Luke 1:39–45), a candle, and a symbol of Mary, the mother of Jesus. (Something as simple as a decorated letter M on a piece of cardboard will do).

Leader   May the peace and love of Jesus be with us today as we gather to talk to God and to listen to God's messages to us.

All   May the peace and love of Jesus be with us.

Leader   During Advent we often hear about Mary, the mother of Jesus. The Gospel stories tell us that she was chosen by God for her special role, and that she received a message from God about it.

Mary wasn't surprised that God should speak to her because she often practiced listening to God. When she realized what God was asking, she simply answered: Whatever you want me to do, my God, I will do it.

Shortly after she found out that she was going to have a baby, she went to visit her cousin Elizabeth who was also pregnant. Here's how Elizabeth greeted Mary:

Reader One   When Elizabeth heard Mary call out in greeting, the baby in her womb jumped. Elizabeth realized at that moment that even her baby knew there was something special about Mary.

Reader Two   Filled with the Holy Spirit, Elizabeth cried out to Mary: "Blessed are you among women and blessed is the baby you are carrying.

The moment your greeting
sounded in my ears,
the baby in my womb jumped for joy.
Blessed are you Mary
for trusting in God's Word to you!" *The Gospel of the Lord.*

All Praise to you, Lord Jesus Christ.

Leader For 2000 years Christians have retold this story, and Mary has become a model of how we should listen to God and trust in God's words to us. In fact, the church has even composed a prayer based on this story. The prayer is called the Hail Mary.

(It might be appropriate at this point to go through the first part of the prayer line by line, rephrasing it in contemporary terms so the children will understand what it means. You might paraphrase it in this way: "Hello, Mary. God has blessed you in a special way, and is always with you. Of all women, you are the most special, and the baby you are carrying is especially blessed by God. In fact, the baby you are carrying is Jesus." You might also explain that the second half of the prayer is not from Scripture. It is a response added much later on.)

Leader We will say this prayer together during each of our Advent classes. It will remind us that we, too, can listen to God in prayer as we prepare to celebrate the birth of Jesus at Christmas.

Now ask children to repeat the Hail Mary after you, line by line.

Leader Hail Mary, full of grace,

All Hail Mary, full of grace,

Leader The Lord is with you.

All The Lord is with you.

Leader Blessed are you among women,

All Blessed are you among women,

Leader And blessed is the fruit of your womb, Jesus.

All And blessed is the fruit of your womb, Jesus.

Leader Holy Mary, Mother of God,

All	Holy Mary, Mother of God,
Leader	Pray for us sinners,
All	Pray for us sinners,
Leader	Now and at the hour of our death.
All	Now and at the hour of our death.
Leader	Amen.
All	Amen.

Before closing, spend two minutes in silent prayer.

Advent Action Encourage children to pray the Hail Mary often during Advent. Suggest that they buy or borrow a rosary (from parents or grandparents) to use for this purpose. If you have a rosary, show it to them and explain briefly how it is used for prayer.

6. Showing Respect

Introduction

Explain to children that Jesus treated every person as a beloved child of God. We are called to do the same, which means allowing each person in the class to be the unique person God has created. Advent is a special time to focus on the teaching that Jesus dwells among us. When we love and respect others we are loving and respecting Jesus. By "others" we mean the very people who are in our lives right now: classmates, teachers, siblings, parents, parish leaders, friends, and neighbors.

To Prepare

Beforehand make small cards for each child with these words written on them: "Remember as you prepare for Christmas: all of God's children deserve our love. Jesus is with ALL of us." Place these in a special container on your prayer table and also place there a votive candle (or your Advent wreath) and a Bible (open to Ephesians 4:32).

Leader   As members of a religion class, we try to have respect for one another, but God calls us to show respect not just for one another, but for everyone. At Christmas we celebrate God's gift of Jesus—who calls all of us "brothers and sisters."

Reader One   In his letter to the Christians at Ephesus, St. Paul wrote: "Be kind to one another and be understanding—as God is understanding with you."

Reader Two   May we honor all people as worthy of our kindness and respect, loving God. May we care for everyone as Jesus did.

All   Help us to show respect to everyone around us, dear God.

Reader Three   Help us to think of others this Advent and to reach out to those in need with true love and concern.

All   Help us to show respect to everyone around us, dear God.

Leader   Let us ask God to guide us as we reflect on how we should treat other people. May we always show respect to one another, to our family members, to our friends and acquaintances, and to all God's children.

Pause for a moment of silent prayer.

Leader   Jesus, you are our Emmanuel, God with us. Teach us how to be faithful followers of your Way—this Advent and always. We ask this through your holy name.

All   Amen.

Advent Action Encourage children to greet every person they meet this Advent with respect. This means listening to others, caring about what concerns them, and believing that every person is a beloved child of God. Have them come forward to the prayer table one by one to draw out one of the cards. After each has received a card, have the children read what it says together.

Optional Activity Place the names of the children in your class in a small bag. Explain to them that they will be drawing names, but the Christmas "present" they will be asked to give does not cost money. It is the gift of respect. Throughout Advent, they should try to do all they can to show respect for the person whose name they have drawn. They should not reveal whose name they have.

On your last class before Christmas, have children try to guess who had their names.

7. Offering Kindness

Introduction

Explain to children that kindness is much more than nice actions toward others. It comes from what is in our hearts. Kind people recognize the inner goodness in all others, not just family members and friends. Encourage children to be kind to others they don't like, to children who are often left out, even to those who have offended them. The gift of kindness is a wonderful gift to share in preparation for Christmas.

To Prepare

Have available a small smooth stone for each child or some other small "reminder" object. Gather around your prayer table on which are placed the stones (or other object), a lighted candle (or your Advent wreath), and a Bible (open to Colossians 3:12–14).

Leader	May this Advent be a time of growth for us. May we practice kindness ourselves and share this gift with all those we meet. Let us listen to what God's Word, the Bible, says about kindness.
Reader One	In his letter to the Christians at Colossae, St. Paul wrote: "Always be merciful in action and kindly in heart. Bear with one another and forgive one another and let the peace of Christ control your hearts." *The Word of the Lord*.
All	Thanks be to God.
Reader Two	Help us, loving God, to see the good qualities in others rather than the bad. Help us to thank and praise others often during this season of Advent.
All	May we be merciful in action and kindly in heart this day.
Reader Three	Help us to be generous in our praise of others, even those who annoy us or make us angry.
All	May we be merciful in action and kindly in heart this day.
Leader	Be with us this day, God our protector and guide. Watch over us at home and at school, and help us to be signs to others of your kindness and love. Let us now pray in silence about our need to practice kindness.
	Pause for a moment of silent prayer.
Leader	You know all our needs, loving God, and so you know that we need your gift of kindness. We make this prayer in Jesus' name.

All   Amen.

Advent Action   Have children come forward one by one to receive their stones (or other reminder objects). As you hand each a stone, say the following: "(Child's name), let this stone remind you to be kind to everyone you meet this day and throughout Advent." Children can respond "Amen."

Encourage children to keep their stones somewhere visible at home as a reminder that they should practice kindness even when it is very difficult to do so. Their acts of kindness can be one of their "gifts" for Jesus at Christmas.

8. Spreading Good Cheer

Introduction

Explain to children that the virtue of cheerfulness or joy is more than smiling and laughing. Cheerful people know that they are God's children in good times and in bad. They know how to rejoice in all the blessings in their lives (and not just when receiving presents). Encourage children to practice giving joy to others as they prepare for the birth of Christ at Christmas.

To Prepare

Have available a piece of posterboard on which these words are written at the top: "We remember these people today. May our prayers give them joy." Also have available crayons or markers. Gather around your prayer table on which are placed a lighted candle (or your class Advent wreath) and a Bible (open to Colossians 3:16).

Leader   As Christians we always have something to be cheerful about because Jesus is with us, not just at Christmas but always. This is good news that we can share with everyone. Let us listen together to what God's Word, the Bible, says about spreading joy.

Reader One   In his letter to the Christians at Colossae, St. Paul wrote: "Teach and help one another through the sharing of psalms and hymns and Christian songs, singing God's praises with cheerful hearts." *The Word of the Lord.*

All   Thanks be to God.

Leader   May we praise God for the gift of Jesus with joy and good cheer.

Reader Two   Guide us this day, loving God, that we might give joy and cheer to others because of our faith in Jesus. Help us when we are tempted to be selfish with our time and our friendship.

All   May we praise God for the gift of Jesus with joy and good cheer.

Reader Three   As we do our chores, work on our school work, play with our friends, and share with our families, may we spread the joy of your presence.

All   May we praise God for the gift of Jesus with joy and good cheer.

Leader   We need God's help to remember that it is Jesus alone who can give us God's good cheer. Let us talk to God in the silence of our hearts about our need to reach out to those most in need of the gift of joy.

Pause for a moment of silent prayer.

Leader	Forgive us, loving God, for our selfish concerns. Help us to think of others, and help us to see Jesus present in everyone we meet. We ask this…
All	In the name of the Father, and of the Son, and of the Holy Spirit. Amen.
Advent Action	Encourage children to think of someone they know who is lonely, sad, or sick. Have them take turns writing the names of these people on the poster. When all the names have been written, invite them to decorate the poster. Then display it somewhere near your prayer table throughout Advent.
Optional Activity	Set up some possible classroom or playground scenarios for role-playing with your class. The goal is to help children become aware of the many opportunities they have to spread cheer to those who need it most. Here are some sample scenarios:

1. Two children want to jump rope, but they need a third child. They can ask someone they like or they can invite a child to play who is often left out. What will they do?

2. A child is asked by the teacher to help with a project that needs two helpers. Who will he choose to help, his best friend or a child who sometimes makes fun of him?

3. An unpopular child needs help with an Advent project, but no one volunteers to help. The teacher appoints someone who is not happy about helping. What should the helper do?

4. Several children are making fun of a girl whose dress is torn, and she starts to cry. Most of the children laugh at her tears, but one steps forward to console her.

9. Waiting with the Saints

Introduction
This service reminds children that saints are people who trust in God and who point the way for us during Advent, but all year through as well. The saints teach children that they, too, can be saints.

To Prepare
In your prayer space, place a Bible (open to Psalm 126), a candle, and, if available, a picture or pictures of saints.

Leader	The grace of our Lord Jesus Christ and the love of God and the fellowship of the Holy Spirit be with you all.
All	And also with you.
Leader	Saints were special people not just because of the great deeds they did, but because they lived good lives. Mostly they lived and died for God and others.
Reader One	The saints put their energy, their intelligence, their talent, and often their material goods at the disposal of God and other people.
Reader Two	Even when life was very hard for them, when there was sickness, or poverty, or suffering of any kind in their lives, the saints praised God.
Reader Three	Psalm 126 says: Those who sow in tears, shall reap with shouts of joy. This means that even though there is sadness in life, when we count on God, we will again rejoice.
Reader Four	Saints are people who have learned to say: "God has done great things for us; we are glad indeed. Although we go forth weeping, carrying the seed to be sown,

we shall come back rejoicing,
carrying our sheaves." *The Word of the Lord.*

All   Thanks be to God.

Leader   Let us now pray to the saints, asking them to guide us during Advent, and asking them, too, to help us live our lives for God and others.

Before you begin, give the children a moment to think of a particular saint they want to pray to. Their name saints would be an obvious choice, but some may not have been named for a saint. Give a few suggestions, so that each child has a saint to pray to. Begin this litany yourself and continue until every child has had a turn.

Leader   Saint Joseph...

All   Pray for us.

Leader   Saint Elizabeth…

Pray for us.

Leader   Saint John the Baptist…

Pray for us.

When all have prayed:

Leader   All you saints of heaven, help us to prepare for the birth of Jesus by loving others as you did. Speak to God for us that we might find joy in giving to others, especially those in need. We ask this in the name of the Father, and of the Son, and of the Holy Spirit.

All   Amen.

Advent Action   Encourage children to ask their parents for whom they were named and to share with them any information about their name saint or the person they were named after.

10. Proclaiming Our Faith

Introduction

Explain to children that Advent is a special time in the church year to think about what a great gift our faith is. Because we care about God and the things of God, we should share our belief in God with others. Faith is one of God's many Christmas gifts to us.

To Prepare

Demonstrate for children how to give someone a blessing (as below). Then gather around your prayer table on which are placed a lighted candle (or your class Advent wreath) and a Bible (open to Ephesians 3:15–19).

Leader	May God bless us today with the gift of faith. May we be on fire with love for Jesus, who cares about us and dwells with us always. Let us listen together to God's Word.
Reader One	In his letter to the Christians in Ephesus, St. Paul wrote: "May God grant you strength through the Holy Spirit and may Christ dwell through faith in your hearts, so that rooted and grounded in love, you may have the fullness of Christ's love." *The Word of the Lord.*
All	Thanks be to God.
Leader	Set our hearts on fire with love for you, Jesus our savior.
Reader Two	May God's love guide us in all our dealings with others. May all who meet us recognize that we are God's beloved children.
All	Set our hearts on fire with love for you, Jesus our savior.
Reader Three	Thank you for the gift of faith, gracious God. Thank you for sending Jesus to dwell among us. May we sing his praises today and always.
All	Set our hearts on fire with love for you, Jesus our savior.
Leader	Let us resolve to remember that Jesus is here with us. May we celebrate his presence with great joy and deep faith. Let us now talk to God in the silence of our hearts about our need to be strong in our faith.
	Pause for a moment of silent prayer.
Leader	We await your coming, Jesus. Set our hearts on fire with love and thanksgiving. We ask this…

All	In the name of the Father, and of the Son, and of the Holy Spirit. Amen.
Advent Action	Invite children to bless one another (by making a sign of the cross on one another's foreheads) with these words: "May your faith in Jesus ever grow stronger." Each can answer "Amen."
Optional Activity	One way that children can learn about their ancestors in the faith is by making a class Jesse Tree. Jesse was the father of King David and Jesus was of "the house of David."

The actual tree can be a large branch anchored in a bucket of sand or a tree shape drawn on a large piece of posterboard. Ask children if they know the names of any other of Jesus' ancestors. Hint: many are written about in the Bible, particularly the Old Testament. Depending on your available class time, have children look up some of the following ancestors in the Bible, and then draw or make something that symbolizes each person: Noah, Abraham, Sarah, Isaac, Rebecca, Jacob, Rachel, Joseph, Moses, Miriam, Jesse, David, Solomon, St. Joseph, Mary, etc.

Hang or paste the finished symbols on your class Jesse Tree and display this throughout Advent.

11. Listening to God

Introduction

Explain to children that Jesus once told his followers that people have ears to hear, but they do not listen. He was talking about REALLY listening with the heart. But even his followers failed to do this. As children prepare to celebrate the birth of Jesus, give them as many opportunities as possible to pray as a class. Invite them to listen in silence to whatever God is asking of them in this Advent season.

To Prepare

Prepare index cards (one for each child) on which these words are printed: "Listen to God." Gather around your prayer table on which are placed the index cards, a lighted candle (or your class Advent wreath) and a Bible (open to Matthew 6:5–7).

Leader	Holy Spirit, you are with us always. Help us to learn from you how to listen to one another and how to listen in the quiet of prayer. Teach us, too, to *really* listen to your holy Word, the Bible.
Reader One	This is what Jesus says about prayer in the Gospel of Matthew: "When you pray, go to your inner room, close the door, and pray to your Father in secret. And your Father who sees in secret will repay you." *The Gospel of the Lord.*
All	Praise to you, Lord Jesus Christ.
Leader	May we hear your Word within our hearts, Holy Spirit.
Reader Two	Forgive us when we have been too busy with our own interests to really hear what others are saying. Forgive us when we have been too busy to hear what you are saying in our minds and hearts.
All	May we hear your Word within our hearts, Holy Spirit.
Reader Three	Teach us, Holy Spirit, how to pray that we might open our minds and hearts to your guidance and help.
All	May we hear your Word within our hearts, Holy Spirit.
Leader	Holy Spirit, bless and watch over us. Help us to love and respect one another and to show this by how we listen. Guide us now as we listen to God in the silence of our hearts.
	Pause for a moment of silent prayer.

Leader As we await the birth of Jesus, may we be open to the many ways that God is speaking to us in our daily lives. We ask this through our Lord, Jesus Christ, who lives and reigns with God now and forever.

All Amen.

Advent Action Encourage children to pause in silence throughout the day to listen for God's Word in their minds and hearts. Before they leave, call them forward one by one and give each child an index card while saying: "(Child's name), let this card remind you to listen to God often." Invite children to take these home as a reminder to practice quiet prayer throughout Advent.

12. Counting Our Blessings

Introduction

Explain to children that generous people freely share their time and talents (as well as money) with others. For Christians, sharing is a very important virtue, one that makes living and working together a joy. Advent is a time to think about what we can share with others, especially those in need.

To Prepare

Have available an envelope for each child as well as slips of paper and pencils. Gather around your prayer table on which are placed a lighted candle (or your class Advent wreath) and a Bible (open to 1 Corinthians 10:24).

Leader	God has given us many blessings to share. We have food and drink; we have our home and furniture; we have our clothes and our personal belongings. May we joyfully share these blessings with others. And may we joyfully share God's Word.
Reader One	When St. Paul wrote the Christians in Corinth, this is what he said: "Let none of us seek only our own good, but rather the good of all."
Leader	We praise your name, our God; you share good things with us.
Reader Two	Thank you, dear God, for giving us many blessings in our lives. Thank you most of all for our families and our parish. May we share love, friendship, and faith this Advent and always.
All	We praise your name, our God; you share good things with us.
Reader Three	Forgive us, loving God, for the times we have forgotten to share. Help us to change and grow as we await the celebration of Jesus' birth. Help us to think of ways we can make others happy.
All	We praise your name, our God; you share good things with us.
Leader	Advent reminds us of God's great generosity in giving us Jesus, who is with us always. Let us each thank God in our own words for this great gift.
	Pause for a moment of silent prayer.
Leader	Thank you for Jesus and for all our gifts, loving God. Help us to share what we have generously. We ask this in Jesus' name.
All	Amen.

Advent Action Invite children to think of something good they can share with someone today, for example, sharing their time by listening or playing with someone who often gets left out, sharing a toy or game at home with a sister or brother, and sharing their love with their parents.

Have them put these intentions on slips of paper inside their envelopes. Add to these throughout Advent until the last class before Christmas when they can take these good deeds home to share with family members.

13. Come Lord Jesus

Introduction

This Advent service focuses on waiting for the birth of Jesus with patience and joy. It compares our Advent waiting with waiting for seeds to take root and grow.

To Prepare

Place on the prayer table a packet of seeds, a container of soil, a Bible (open to James 5:7–10), and a votive candle (or your class Advent wreath). Optional: if possible, also place a blooming plant on your prayer table.

Leader	Peace be with you, children.
All	And also with you.
Leader	During this season of Advent, we wait and prepare for the birthday of Jesus. Because we know that we will get presents at Christmas, and have parties, and maybe even have company from out of town, it is very hard to wait. So we must have patience. Do you know what patience is? (pause for answers) How does it "feel" to be patient? (pause) For what jobs must people be very patient?
	Invite children to discuss their concepts of waiting and patience, and to guess which grown-up occupations require the most patience.
Leader	Farmers are certainly people who know what patience feels like. All winter long they have to wait until the soil is ready again for seeds and plants. And after they plant in spring, they must wait for the seeds to grow and produce.
	Did you know that during Advent, one of the Sunday readings is about farmers (Third Sunday of Advent)? Here's what it says.
Reader One	A reading from the letter of James: Be patient my brothers and sisters, until the coming of the Lord. Look at the farmers. See how they wait for their crops to grow until they can be gathered.
Reader Two	They have to wait patiently while the soil receives the winter and the spring rains. You, too, must be patient. Steady your hearts, because Jesus is coming soon.

Do not grumble among yourselves,
but instead, practice patience.
The Word of the Lord.

All   Thanks be to God.

Leader   Let us now pray to God, our loving parent, as we wait for the coming of Jesus.

Reader Three   That we might learn from those who farm the land
how to wait with patience, let us pray to the Lord…

All   Lord, hear our prayer.

Reader Four   That we might use our Advent waiting time to prepare our hearts for the birthday of Jesus, let us pray to the Lord…

All   Lord, hear our prayer.

Reader Five   That we might remember when we share gifts on Christmas that God first shared the gift of Jesus with us, let us pray to the Lord…

All   Lord, hear our prayer.

Reader Six   That we might think first of Jesus on Christmas morning, remembering that it is his birthday, let us pray to the Lord…

All   Lord, hear our prayer.

Leader   Let us now add our own prayers to these.

Invite children to pray for personal or family needs, or about any concerns they may have. When all who wish have prayed, continue as below.

Leader   (holding up the packet of seeds and the soil) God, our loving parent, thank you for Jesus. Thank you for the farmers who work the land, and thank you for the gift of patience. May Jesus come soon. Come, Lord Jesus, come. Amen.

All   Come, Lord Jesus, come. Amen.

Advent Action   Invite children to come forward one at a time to place a seed in the soil. If possible, keep the container in a sunny place and have children check the progress of the seeds each time you gather.

14. Recognizing Jesus

Introduction

Explain to children that through the gift of faith we place our lives in God's hands, believing that God will guide us. God sent Jesus to show us the way. This is what we really celebrate at Christmas.

To Prepare

Have available pencils and small cards for each child on which the word "FAITH" is printed vertically. Gather around your prayer table on which are placed a lighted candle (or your Advent wreath) and a Bible (open to Philippians 2:11).

Leader	Help us, loving God, to grow in faith this Advent. Please strengthen our faith to recognize that Jesus is here with us, always loving and guiding us. Teach us how to listen to your Word.
Reader One	St. Paul wrote this to the Christians at Philippi: "Every tongue shall confess that Jesus Christ is the Lord, which gives glory to God the Father."
Leader	Thank you for the gift of Jesus, loving God.
Reader Two	We believe that Jesus is our savior, who not only watches over us, but also calls us forward to do good things for others.
All	Thank you for the gift of Jesus, loving God.
Reader Three	We believe that when we gather for prayer, Jesus is here in our midst.
All	Thank you for the gift of Jesus, loving God.
Leader	Believing that God listens to our prayers and does what is best for us, let us now ask God in our own words to make our faith even stronger.
	Pause for a moment of silent prayer.
Leader	Let us end our prayer by giving praise to God.
All	Glory be to the Father, and to the Son, and to the Holy Spirit, as it was in the beginning, is now, and ever shall be, world without end. Amen.
Advent Action	Give each child one of the cards and challenge each to find a word that describes faith for each of the letters F-A-I-T-H. For example, F is for firm, A is for always, I is for "I believe," T is for true, and H is for "from the Heart." Have children share these at home with their family members.

15. Learning to Love

Introduction

Explain to children that love is more than words and showing affection. People who really love others are willing to do things, even difficult things, for those they love. That's how Jesus' love is for us. Advent is a time in the church year to reflect on the meaning of God's great love for us in giving us Jesus to be with us always.

To Prepare

Have available a poster on which these words are written at the top: "Love is…. " Gather around your prayer table on which are placed a lighted candle (or your class Advent wreath) and a Bible (open to 1 Corinthians 13:13 or 1 John 4:7).

Leader	Guide us, God of Love, as we continue on our Advent journey. You teach us in scripture that love is the greatest of all gifts. Help us to practice it during Advent so that we might love others as you want us to love them. Open our minds and hearts to your Word.
Reader One	Scripture says: "There are in the end three things that last: faith, hope, and love, and the greatest of these is love." It also says: "Beloved, let us love one another because God is love." *The Word of the Lord.*
All	Thanks be to God.
Leader	Let us love one another because God is love.
Reader Two	You tell us, Jesus, that those who practice charity are patient and kind. They are not jealous and do not show off.
All	Let us love one another because God is love.
Reader Three	You teach us, Jesus, that loving people are never rude or selfish, and they don't carry grudges.
All	Let us love one another because God is love.
Leader	Thank you for this wonderful gift, loving God. Help us to practice it all through Advent, at home, at school, in religion class, and everywhere we go. Let us now talk to God in silence about our need to grow in love.
	Pause for a moment of silent prayer.
Leader	Thank you for the gift of Jesus and thank you for the gift of love, dear God. May we share it often. We pray this in Jesus' name…

All   Amen.

Advent Action   Read to the children St. Paul's complete definition of love in the first letter
to the Corinthians (chapter 13:4–7). Then invite each child to consider how
to complete the sentence "Love is…" on your poster. One by one, have
them write their definition on the poster. (Write your own as well.)

Encourage children to take this message home by asking family members
how they define love.

16. Jesus Is among Us

Introduction

This service focuses on the presence of Jesus among us, which we celebrate at Christmas. It invites children to think of Advent as a time to prepare for and rejoice in the presence of our savior who is always with us, loving us and calling us forth from our sins. It might work best with older children who can more readily see a connection between the birth of Jesus and our Christian call to reveal him in our daily lives.

To Prepare

Have available slips of paper and pencils for each child. Place on your prayer table a Bible (open to John 1:14–16), a candle (or your class Advent wreath), and a container (a basket or bowl).

Leader	Jesus, we have gathered together on this Advent day to celebrate your presence among us. The real gift of Christmas is that God loved us enough to share you with us. Teach us to recognize this great gift and to grow in our understanding of it. Forgive us for the times we have ignored you and been ungrateful for the great gift of faith.
Reader One	The Word became flesh and dwelt among us, and we have seen his glory: the glory of an only Son coming from the Father, filled with enduring love....Of his fullness we have all had a share—love heaped upon love....No one has ever seen God. The only Son, who is in the bosom of the Father, it is he who has revealed God to us. *The Gospel of the Lord.*
All	Praise to you, Lord Jesus Christ.
Reader Two	As Christians we ask ourselves: What difference does it make that Jesus was born all those years ago, if we do not give birth to him through our actions every day of our lives? Jesus is among us, his followers, and we are the ones who must show his presence in our own day and age.
Reader One	Jesus reveals God to us, and we reveal Jesus to others. This is a great mystery. God has given us a great task. But how can we do it? We are weak human beings who are selfish and sinful. How can we reveal Jesus to others?
Reader Two	Because we are human, we are sinners as well as saints. God knows us as we are and loves us just the same. It is the gift of God's forgiveness that enables us to proclaim Jesus. We are weak and selfish, but we can be forgiven. When we share with others the good news that our God is among us, loving and forgiving, we are revealing Jesus.

Leader	Let's think together about these things now in the silence of our hearts. Close your eyes and listen carefully. Think of something you did in the past for which you were particularly sorry. Was it something you did or said to your parents? Was it something you did or said to a friend? How did you feel afterward? Did you ever talk to your parents or your friend about what you did? Even if you didn't, you can talk to Jesus about it now.
	Picture Jesus sitting in your living room at home waiting for you. His eyes light up when he sees you walk in. Talk to him about what you have done in the past. Share with him any problems or weaknesses you are feeling right now. Ask him for forgiveness.
	Allow sufficient time for this, two minutes or so.
Leader	Jesus, we know that you dwell among us and that we celebrate this great mystery at Christmas. We are preparing for it now during Advent. Because we are often distracted and selfish, however, we forget that you are with us and we forget what Advent is all about. Help us to remember that you are with us always. We ask this…
All	…in the name of the Father, and of the Son, and of the Holy Spirit. Amen.
Advent Action	Give out the slips of paper and invite children to write in their own words one item for a class code of Advent behavior. In other words, what do they think is required of them in order to reveal Jesus to others this Advent?
	When all have written an item, have them place them in the container on the prayer table. In future classes, hold up the container during prayertime and remind children of their call to reveal Jesus to others in their daily lives.

17. Spreading Peace

Introduction

Explain to children that peace is a gift we all hope for. It is the ability to feel God's presence in our lives, no matter what. Jesus promised at the last supper to give us this special gift. During Advent we focus on the coming of the Prince of Peace, a special title the church uses for Jesus.

To Prepare

Have available heavy paper, precut in pieces 2"x6", pens, markers, or crayons. Practice with children how to offer one another a sign of peace using the words, "May the peace of Christ be with you." Then gather around your prayer table on which are placed a lighted candle (or your class Advent wreath) and a Bible (open to John 14:27).

Leader	Holy Spirit, please teach us how to live in peace. We need your help to be peaceful people who offer only good things to those we meet in our daily lives. Please forgive us for the times we have not offered peace to others. Help us now to open our hearts to your Word.
Reader One	Jesus said to his friends and followers: "Peace is my farewell gift to you, my peace I give to you. But I do not give it to you as the world gives peace." *The Gospel of the Lord.*
All	Praise to you, Lord Jesus Christ.
Leader	May the peace of Christ be with us always.
Reader Two	Just as Jesus said, "My peace I leave you; my peace I give to you," may each of us be bearers of peace this day.
All	May the peace of Christ be with us always.
Reader Three	Help us to be people of peace at school with classmates and teachers, here in our religion class, in our parish church during Mass, and at home with our families.
All	May the peace of Christ be with us always.
Leader	May there be peace in our hearts today and all through Advent. In silence, let us now talk to God in our own words about our need to share the gift of peace.
	Pause for a moment of silent prayer.

Leader   Let there be peace on Earth, Holy Spirit, especially in the hearts of those who are suffering and sad. Let there be peace in our hearts. We ask this in Jesus' name.

All   Amen.

Advent Action   Give children the paper, etc., and invite them to make simple peace bookmarks for someone who might need the gift of peace. They can use and decorate words like: Peace be with you; Give us peace, Jesus; and Share God's gift of peace. At the end of class, invite children to offer one another a sign of peace.

Encourage them to offer this greeting to each family member at bedtime throughout Advent.

Encourage them, too, to actually give the bookmarks they have made to someone they know who needs a boost.

18. Showing Our Thanks

Introduction

Explain to children that when we give thanks often, to God and to others, we grow in appreciation of ordinary things. Thanksgiving fills us with joy. Advent is a wonderful time to say thank you to all those who make our lives pleasant. Remind children that gift-giving need not be limited to material gifts. We can also share spiritual gifts with those around us. One of these is thanksgiving.

To Prepare

Have available pieces of paper and pencils for each child. Gather around your prayer table on which are placed a lighted candle (or your class Advent wreath), a Bible (open to Colossians 3:15), and a special container (a basket or bowl will suffice, but you may want to have a box wrapped with Christmas paper that has a slit in the top).

Leader	We praise you, God, for all the wonders in our lives. Help us to be grateful for all that we have received. Help us to listen with thanksgiving to your Word.
Reader One	In his letter to the Christians at Colossae, St. Paul wrote: "Let Christ rule your hearts…and never forget to be thankful for what God has done for you." *The Word of the Lord.*
All	Thanks be to God.
Leader	Holy God, may we praise and thank you always.
Reader Two	Help us to notice the good things others do for us, and help us to do good things for others as we prepare for Christmas.
All	Holy God, may we praise and thank you always.
Reader Three	Help us to notice the good qualities of our parents and teachers and to thank them often and to thank God for giving us their love and care.
All	Holy God, may we praise and thank you always.
Reader Three	Help us to notice and give thanks for the wonderful qualities of our classmates and friends. Help us to look for the good qualities in everyone we meet.
All	Holy God, may we praise and thank you always.
Leader	Let us thank God often during this Advent season for the many simple and

beautiful gifts in our lives. Let us now talk to God in silence about our need for the gift of thanksgiving.

Pause for a moment of silent prayer.

Leader   Thank you, Holy God, for all your gifts and in particular for the gift of one another. We pray this in Jesus' name.

All   Amen.

Advent Action   Invite children to write a brief thank you note to God listing some of the things for which they are particularly grateful. When all are completed, place them in the special container on your prayer table. Every Advent prayertime thereafter, have one of the children hold the container as a sign of their thanks to God.

19. Showing Our Joy

Introduction

Explain to children that joy is more than a feeling; it is knowing that we are God's children and that God loves us very much. God wants us to share this joy with everyone in our lives, not just during Advent but all year through. Our culture wants us to believe that real joy comes from more and more presents. Scripture tells us that true joy comes from God.

To Prepare

Have available slips of paper on which one of these five statements is printed:

> Smile at someone who is sad today;
>
> Make someone happy with a phone call;
>
> Tell your parents that you love them;
>
> Say thank you to everyone who helps you today;
>
> Say something nice to someone who is lonely.

Place these in a container on your prayer table, as well as a lighted candle (or your Advent wreath) and a Bible (open to Philippians 4:5).

Leader   God of Joy, help us to remember that you want us to be happy people and you want us to give joy to others at Christmastime and always. Help us to joyously listen to your Word.

Reader One   In his letter to the Christians at Philippi, St. Paul wrote: "Delight yourselves in the Lord; yes, find your joy in God at all times. Everyone should see how happy you are because the Lord is near." *The Word of the Lord.*

All   Thanks be to God.

Leader   May we delight in God in everything we do.

Reader Two   At school and in religion class this Advent, help us to reach out to those who are sad and ignored. Help us to offer them joy and make them smile.

All   May we delight in God in everything we do.

Reader Three   At home this Advent, help us to do our share to lighten the burdens of others and so to give them joy.

All   May we delight in God in everything we do.

Leader   On the playground, in the classroom, in our neighborhood, at home, and anywhere else we are today, may we remind others that our God wants us to rejoice and be happy. Let us now talk to God in our own words about our need for the gift of joy.

Pause for a moment of silent prayer.

Leader   May our Advent journey take us closer and closer to the heart of God where we will find joy beyond measure. We ask this…

All   In the name of the Father, and of the Son, and of the Holy Spirit, Amen.

Advent Action   Invite children one by one to draw out one of the slips in your container. Have them read these silently and encourage them to do what is on the slip. (Have them ask for help from parents if they're not sure how to do the action.) Also remind them that wherever they are today, they should watch for those who need the gift of a smile—and freely share one with them.

20. Learning Patience

Introduction

Explain to children that everyone needs the gift of patience. This gift helps us to accept one another as we are and not as we want one another to be. Encourage them to practice being patient during the remaining days of Advent, and point out that the gift of patience is a wonderful Christmas gift to give others.

To Prepare

Have available large Christmas tags (one for each child) or paper to make tags, pencils, and markers or crayons. Place on your prayer table a candle (or your Advent wreath), and a Bible (open to Colossians 3:12).

Leader	Oh God, you love us so much and you are so patient with us. Even when again and again we fail to do the right thing, you are patient with us. Help us to be as patient with one another. Let us listen now to what the Bible says about patience.
Reader One	Scripture says: "Beloved of God, accept life as it is and be very patient with one another. Try to put up with one another and always be ready to forgive." *The Word of the Lord.*
All	Thanks be to God.
Leader	God has promised us that Jesus is with us always. Sometimes we forget this and give in to bad habits like anger, greed, and impatience.
All	You are always with us, Jesus. Give us patience and joy.
Reader Two	Help us to be patient today with one another, with our teachers and classmates, and with our friends and neighbors.
All	You are always with us, Jesus. Give us patience and joy.
Reader Three	Help us to be patient enough to recognize you today, Jesus, so that you may be born anew in us.
All	You are always with us, Jesus. Give us patience and joy.
Leader	In the quiet of our prayer, we can learn to wait for God with patience. Let us wait on God now, opening our minds and hearts to whatever God wants to say to us.

Pause for a moment of silent prayer.

Leader	Help us, loving God, to be patient in the days remaining before Christmas. Help us to think of ways to give joy to others as we wait. We ask this in Jesus' name.
All	Amen.
Advent Action	Give each child one of the tags (or supplies to make tags), and have them write the person's name on it who most needs the gift of patience from them, for example, a mother or father, a younger sibling, or a classmate. They should put their own name under "from."

Encourage children to take these home and keep them in a visible place as a reminder of their need to practice patience. |
| **Optional Activity** | Place on your prayer table or desk a gift-wrapped box with prayer cards inside (from you, one for each child). To make these cards you will need posterboard, Christmas stickers, religious ones if available, and a black pen. On each write: Remember, Jesus is with you always!

Before they leave, have children gather around the prayer table (or your desk) to open your "gift." Give each child one of the cards and explain that the best gift you can give them is a reminder of the presence of Jesus—our greatest ever Christmas gift. |

21. Saying Thanks

Introduction

God gives us many good gifts us of nature and we often take them for granted. The children in our classes often equate "gifts" with material possessions only, so it's very important to point out the many other kinds of gifts that God gives us. Explain that the days before Christmas are ideal for reflecting on God's gifts.

To Prepare

Discuss with children beforehand what "gifts of nature" they are aware of. Invite them to bring to this service a symbol of some created thing for which they are particularly grateful. Or invite them to draw a picture of something they enjoy in nature. With these items in hand, have the children walk in procession to your prayer space, holding high their nature symbols or drawings. When they reach the prayer space, invite them to place what they are carrying on the prayer table. Place a lighted candle in the center (or your class Advent wreath) beside a Bible (open to Psalm 66).

Leader	Together let us "shout out" our thanks to God for all the wonderful things in nature that we enjoy. Sometimes we forget that things like sunshine, flowers, clouds, grass, water, sand, and snow are all gifts from God. (In a loud voice:) Let us thank God for all the gifts of nature.
All	Let us thank God for all the gifts of nature.
Reader One	We give you thanks, God of all creation, for the gifts of sun, moon, and stars, for planets and galaxies, for ages past and ages to come…
All	We give you thanks, great and generous God.
Reader Two	We give you thanks, God of all creation, for snow and ice, for bare winter trees, for snow-covered hillsides and frozen lakes, glistening in the sun…
All	We give you thanks, almighty and all knowing God.
Reader Three	We give you thanks, God of all creation, for the wind and the water, the beach and the sand… for the clouds in the sky, for sunrises and sunsets…

All	We give you thanks, loving and caring God.
Reader Four	We give you thanks, God of all creation, for the gift of rain that waters the earth… for birds and fish, and all the creatures of the sea and sky… for animals and for all the fruits of the land…
All	We give you thanks, gracious and good God.
	(Invite children to add to this list some of the things in nature they enjoy.)
Leader	We ask you, God, to help us value and take care of the gifts you have given us. Let us each in our own way talk to God now about gifts of nature we enjoy.
	Pause for a moment of silent prayer.
Leader	Help us to keep our Earth safe and clean. Thank you for all the gifts you have given us, loving God, this Advent and always. We pray this in Jesus' name…
All	Amen.
Advent Action	Invite children to go one by one to the prayer table to pick up their symbols or drawings. Encourage any who wish to do so to tell the others about what they have brought [or drawn].
	When all have had a turn, encourage the children to take their symbols or drawings home to share with family members.

22. Preparing for Christmas

Introduction

This service is intended to help children think about the true meaning of Christmas. Beforehand ask them to name some ways that our culture distracts us from the true meaning of Christmas (for example, too much emphasis on spending money, secular Christmas music, Christmas cards that don't mention Christ, commercials telling us to buy more and more presents, etc.).

To Prepare

Beforehand, prepare a card for each child on which these words are printed: "Jesus was born on Christmas day; let us celebrate and rejoice!" Place these on your prayer table as well as a candle (or your Advent wreath) and a birthday card. (Optional: You might want to bake a birthday cake or cupcakes, and these, too, can be placed on the prayer table.)

Leader	Jesus was born on Christmas day. Let us celebrate with him. Let us rejoice with him.
All	On Christmas day we celebrate and rejoice with Jesus.
Reader One	On Christmas day we celebrate the greatest gift that God ever gave us. We celebrate the gift of Jesus. In imitation of God's giving, we give one another gifts.
All	On Christmas day we celebrate and rejoice with Jesus.
Reader Two	On Christmas day God is saying: This birthday of Jesus is the greatest birthday of all. All of you should celebrate and rejoice.
Leader	Jesus was born on Christmas day. All of us can celebrate! All of us can rejoice!
All	On Christmas day we celebrate and rejoice with Jesus.
Leader	Here on our prayer table is a birthday card. Let's take a few minutes to read it, and then all of us can sign it. Even though we can't really mail it to Jesus, it will remind us that Christmas is his birthday.

Read the card together. Sign it yourself and then have the children sign it. Then have one child hold the card high as you pray the following.

Leader   Jesus was born on Christmas day.

All   Jesus was born on Christmas day.

Leader   All of us can celebrate!

All   All of us can celebrate!

Leader   All of us can rejoice!

All   All of us can rejoice!

Leader   Thank you, God, for the gift of Jesus. Amen.

All   Thank you, God, for the gift of Jesus. Amen.

**Christmas
Action**   Before the children leave, distribute the cards to them with these words: "Remember the great gift God has given us."

**Optional
Activity**   Now share the cake or cupcakes.

23. Offering Our Gifts

Introduction

Though you will very likely not have class on the feast of Epiphany, this service celebrates the visit of the magi (also know as the Three Kings) and encourages children to think of ways they can offer gifts to Jesus.

To Prepare

Beforehand draw a large crown on a piece of poster-board and beneath it print: Jesus Is the Center of Our Lives. Leave room for "gems" to be added to the crown. Also using posterboard, cut out gem shapes, one for each child. Have available pencils and tape. Place the gems on your prayer table in a container, as well as a Bible (open to Matthew 2:1–12) and a votive candle.

Leader	Guide us, God of the Ages, as we continue our journey through the Christmas season. We look forward to the celebration of Epiphany when we reflect on the story of the three wise men. Though they were weary from their long journey, they bowed low before Jesus and offered him wonderful gifts.
All	What can we give you, Christ our king? When we come to you, what can we bring?
Reader One	One king offered Jesus gold, a very expensive gift that was a sign of the future greatness of this child.
All	What can we give you, Christ our king? When we come to you, what can we bring?
Reader Two	The second king offered frankincense, a resin used to make perfumes and incense. This was a sign that Jesus would someday be a wise and respected leader.
All	What can we give you, Christ our king? When we come to you, what can we bring?
Reader Three	The third king offered myrrh, a sweet-smelling herb that was sometimes placed in burial cloths. This was a sign that Jesus would die in a remarkable way.

All	What can we give you, Christ our king? When we come to you, what can we bring?
Leader	Let us now listen to what God's Word says about these three special visitors.
Reader Four	A reading from the Gospel of Matthew. When Jesus was born in Bethlehem of Judea, in the days of King Herod, behold magi from the east arrived in Jerusalem saying, "Where is the newborn king of the Jews? We saw his star at its rising and have come to do him homage...."
Reader Five	And behold, the star that they had seen at its rising preceded them, until it came and stopped over the place where the child was. They were overjoyed at seeing the star, and on entering they saw the child and did him homage. Then they opened their treasures and offered him gifts of gold, frankincense, and myrrh. *The Gospel of the Lord.*
All	Praise to you, Lord Jesus Christ.
Leader	The feast of the three kings, which we also call Epiphany, reminds us that Jesus is at the center of our lives. He is our king, our savior, our leader, and our redeemer. Let us now talk to him in our own words about our need for his love and care.
	Pause for a moment of silent prayer.
Leader	Thank you for the gift of Jesus, dear God, and thank you for this feast that reminds us of how lucky we are to have Jesus in our lives. Help us to give him our love, our praise, and our attention throughout this Christmas season and always.
All	What can we give you, Jesus our king? When we come to you, what can we bring? Teach us to love you and serve you in others, to share what we have with our sisters and brothers. Amen.
Epiphany Action	Ask children to think of one thing they can do for Jesus today (by doing something for someone Jesus loves). Have them write this action on the backside of one of the "gems" and then tape the gem on the crown. Remind children to actually *do* what they have written—as an Epiphany gift to Jesus.

Part Two: The Season of Lent

Lent is a season of prayer, fasting (or penance), and self-giving (or almsgiving). It begins on Ash Wednesday and culminates in the joyful celebration of Christ's victory over sin and death at Easter. In the early church those who were to be initiated into full membership in the Christian community fasted during Lent as a preparation for the sacraments. At first the time of actual fasting was only two days, but by the fourth century an extended fast of forty days was usual.

Three practices often recommended during Lent are prayer, fasting, and almsgiving. All three, of course, can be practiced throughout the year, but Lent is an excellent time to renew ourselves spiritually through these and other practices. You will want the children you teach to know that these three practices are important ways to observe Lent. Prayer keeps us in communication with God, fasting (or sacrifice) helps us to be strong enough to avoid temptation and sin, and almsgiving (or service) helps us to relate to all other people as sons and daughters of God.

Prayer in particular should receive our attention during Lent, since without it we are not communicating with God. Prayer has been defined in many ways: as the lifting of the mind and heart to God; as an intimate conversation with God; as a heart-to-heart talk with God; as silent listening, etc. However we define it, when we spend time in prayer we are keeping in touch with God and allowing God to keep in touch with us.

That is the goal of the services in this section. Note that there are also several services for the Easter season and Pentecost. The mysteries celebrated at these great feasts are what our lenten journey moves toward.

1. We Prepare for Lent

Introduction

Lent offers us and our children an opportunity to renew our baptismal promise to follow Jesus. We can look at our lives to determine if we are following Jesus faithfully or if we have developed habits that take us away from our Christian commitment. In this service the focus is on renewing our baptismal promises in order to follow Jesus more closely. (The wording of the promises is adapted for children.)

To Prepare

Place on your prayer table a Bible (open to Luke 24:50–53), a votive candle, a container (a basket or bowl), a small jar of holy water, and any baptismal items you may have on hand, for example: a baptismal candle, "robe," or certificate. For the Lenten Action, you will need pencils, small cards, and holy water.

Leader	Jesus, you have called us to follow you from the moment of baptism until now. As we enter the season of Lent, help us to think about our Christian faith and to see if we are living it the best we can. Please give us your help and send your Holy Spirit to guide us. We ask these things…
All	…in the name of the Father, and of the Son, and of the Holy Spirit. Amen.
Leader	When we were babies, our parents and godparents made promises in our name. Now that we are older, we can renew these promises ourselves. We can take responsibility for our call to follow Jesus.
Reader One	Our parents and godparents promised at baptism to turn our lives over to Jesus. Now we can do so on our own.
Leader	Will you try this Lent to put yourself in Jesus' hands?
All	We will try this Lent to put ourselves in Jesus' hands.
Reader Two	When we were baptized, our parents and godparents asked forgiveness for our sins and they asked the church to pour the cleansing waters of baptism over us. Now we can ask forgiveness on our own.
Leader	Are you sorry for your sins and failings?
All	We are sorry for our sins and failings.
Reader Three	When we were baptized, our parents and godparents promised to help us reject all that is sinful and to reject Satan who tempts us to stray from Jesus.

Leader	Will you try to resist temptation and to follow Jesus closely?
All	We will try to resist temptation and to follow Jesus closely.
Reader Four	Our parents and godparents also promised to raise us in our Catholic faith, to believe in God, Father, Son, and Holy Spirit, and to place our faith in the teachings of the church. Now we can do this on our own.
Leader	Do you believe in God, the Father, Son, and Holy Spirit, and in the teachings of the church?
All	We believe in God and in the teachings of the church.
Leader	We have now said in our own voices that we will try to love and follow Jesus. Jesus who is here with us now. Close your eyes and picture him sitting near you. Reach out in your imagination and take his hand and tell him what is in your heart. Ask him questions about your baptism; ask him to explain anything you don't understand. Then be still and listen to his voice in your mind and heart.
	Allow two to three minutes for silent prayer.
Leader	Jesus, you have called us to come and follow you. Help us to remember during the coming season of Lent that you are with us always. We ask these things in your holy name.
All	Amen.
Lenten Action	Give children the cards and invite them to write a brief prayer to Jesus that expresses their desire to follow him more closely. When all have written something, invite them forward one at a time to place their cards in the container on your prayer table, and then bless each child with the holy water while saying: "(Child's name), remember your baptism with joy." Each time you pray as a class during Lent, have one of the children hold up the container as a reminder of their prayers.

2. Keeping Close to God

Introduction

This service emphasizes the importance of prayer and encourages children to examine their prayer habits. It teaches them to rely on Jesus to lead them to God, during Lent and always.

To Prepare

Place on your prayer table a Bible (open to John 14:1,18–19), a votive candle, and a chart that says "Lent" in large letters.

Leader	Jesus, you were sent from God to show us the way to God. Teach us how to pray. Teach us how to talk to God by placing ourselves next to you. You have promised that if we believe in you, you will dwell with us. When you dwell with us, so does God. Teach us to believe this, and teach us to pray. We ask this…
All	…in the name of the Father, and of the Son, and of the Holy Spirit. Amen.
Reader One	A reading from the Gospel of John: "Do not be worried and upset," Jesus told his followers, "just believe in God, and believe also in me. I will not leave you alone; I will come back to you. In a little while the world will see me no more, but you will see me; and because I live, you also will live. When that day comes, you will know that I am in my Father, and that you are in me, just as I am in you." *The Gospel of the Lord.*
All	Praise to you, Lord Jesus Christ.
Reader Two	Jesus said, "I will not leave you alone; I will come back to you."
All	Help us to believe, Jesus.
Reader Two	Because he lives, we also will live.
All	Help us to believe, Jesus.
Reader Two	He is with us, just as we are with him.
All	Help us to believe, Jesus.
Leader	Sometimes it's difficult for us to believe that God loves us this much. Imagine being given the gift of Jesus! The question for us is: How do we respond to Jesus? Do we talk to him often and ask for his guidance? Or do we ignore him altogether?
	Close your eyes now and imagine yourself in a place you like to go by

yourself. Picture Jesus there in that place waiting for you. Go and sit beside him. Tell him what's on your mind right now. Are you worried about anything? Tell him. Are you excited about something? Tell him. Are you sorry for something you have done? Tell him and ask for his forgiveness. Now just sit quietly and listen to whatever Jesus wants to say to you.

Allow two to three minutes for silent prayer.

Leader Jesus, help us to remember that you are with us always. Strengthen our faith in God and in you.

All We believe in God, we believe in you; help our unbelief, Jesus. Amen.

Lenten Action Place the chart that says "Lent" in front of the children. Invite them to brainstorm about where, when, and how they can observe Lent during the coming week. Then have each child come forward to write a word or draw a symbol of what they hope to do. If possible, keep this poster in a visible place throughout Lent and have children add to it as often as they wish.

3. Learning to Pray

Introduction

When the disciples asked Jesus how they should pray, he gave them the words of the Our Father. This is a beautiful prayer for Lent and because it is so familiar it is a good one to recommend to children for their daily prayer.

To Prepare

Place on your prayer table a Bible (open to Matthew 6:9–13), a votive candle, and copies of the Our Father, one for each child.

Leader   Jesus, our savior, teach us how to talk to God, to spend time being quiet so we can listen to God, to praise and thank God, to ask for what we need, and to express our sorrow when we have hurt others.

Reader One   When the followers of Jesus asked him how they should pray, he told them: "Pray this way: Our Father who art in heaven, hallowed be thy name..."

All   Thy kingdom come, thy will be done, on earth as it is in heaven.

Reader Two   Jesus, our brother, teach us to ask for our daily bread and to give thanks for it by sharing it with those in need. Forgive us when we fail and teach us to forgive others as you forgive us.

All   Give us this day our daily bread, and forgive us our trespasses as we forgive those who trespass against us.

Reader Three   Jesus, our friend, strengthen us to avoid evil and to turn away from anyone who leads us away from you.

All   And lead us not into temptation, but deliver us from evil.

Leader   May we someday be with Jesus in your kingdom, God, our God, and may we be signs of your love and care today and through this lenten season. Teach us now in the silence of our hearts how to pray.

Pause for a moment of silent prayer.

Leader   As Jesus taught us, let us now pray together…

All   Our Father, who art in heaven,
                    hallowed be thy name.
                    Thy kingdom come, thy will be done
                    on earth as it is in heaven.
                    Give us this day our daily bread,
                    and forgive us our trespasses
                    as we forgive those who trespass against us.
                    And lead us not into temptation,
                    but deliver us from evil. Amen.

Lenten Action   Call children forward one by one and give each a copy of the Our Father.
                    Encourage them to say it two or three more times before this day is over,
                    and to invite family members to pray it with them at home.

4. Needing God

Introduction

Lent is a special time in the church year to focus on our need for God. Jesus knows (and loves) what is in our hearts and is always ready to call us forward, in spite of our weaknesses.

To Prepare

Place on your prayer table a Bible (open to John 13:21–33,36–38), a votive candle, pencils, slips of paper, one for each child, and a container (basket or bowl).

Leader	Jesus knew and loved his first followers, just as he knows and loves us today. We say that we believe in him and want to follow him, but we make mistakes. May Jesus forgive us as he forgave his apostles.
Reader One	Scripture says that at the Last Supper Jesus became very sad and his followers all noticed it. Finally he said to them, "I have to tell you something that troubles me very much. One of you is going to betray me this very night."
All	Lord Jesus Christ, son of the living God, have mercy on us.
Reader Two	Forgive us, Jesus, when we are rude or impatient with one another. Forgive us when we are selfish or disrespectful.
All	Lord Jesus Christ, son of the living God, have mercy on us.
Reader Three	Forgive us when we hurt the feelings of our family members or act mean toward our classmates or teachers, and forgive us when we disappoint our friends.
All	Lord Jesus Christ, son of the living God, have mercy on us.
Leader	Jesus, you knew that Judas would betray you on the night of the Last Supper, and you knew that Peter would deny that he ever knew you. And yet, you loved them. Thank you that you love us, too.
	Pause for a moment of silent prayer.
Leader	During this Lent, Jesus, may we talk to you often about our need for strength and courage to love and serve others in your name. We believe in you, Jesus; please strengthen our faith.
All	Lord Jesus Christ, son of the living God, have mercy on us. Amen.

Lenten Action   Give children the slips of paper and a pencil and have them write on the paper (anonymously) one fault that is keeping them from following Jesus. Collect these in the container from your prayer table (without reading them) and holding them high say aloud: Lord Jesus Christ, forgive us for these and all our sins. Then visibly place the papers in a wastebasket as a sign that our faults are forgotten and forgiven.

Optional Activity   Have children read the entire account in John 13:21–35 of Jesus' words to his followers. Invite children to choose one of the characters in this account (Jesus, Judas, Peter, John) and then to write a paragraph describing how they think that character felt.

5. Looking for Jesus

Introduction

This service helps children reflect on the presence of Jesus here and now. It leads them to the gospel teaching that how they relate to those around them is how they relate to Jesus. It is ideal for helping them examine their behavior toward others. Explain before the service that sin upsets the balance of our relationship with God and Jesus. To make that relationship "right" (in other words, to be reconciled with God and Jesus), we must balance our relationships with the people around us.

To Prepare

Have available paper, crayons or markers, and tape for the Lenten Action. Place a votive candle and a Bible (open to John 16), on your prayer table.

Leader	Jesus, you are here with us. You promised your followers that you would never leave them, and that promise extends to us, too. You are here with us through your Holy Spirit. We don't see your Spirit, but our faith tells us that your Spirit is real. Fill our hearts with love as we now pray and think together about our relationship with you.
Reader One	After he died on the cross and was raised to new life, Jesus ascended to heaven. Before he left, he promised his followers that he would remain with them always. He would send them a helper and friend to keep his presence alive. But the followers wondered: how can we know that Jesus is with us if we can't see him? They gathered together in the Upper Room to pray about this.
All	Help us to believe that you are with us, Jesus.
Reader Two	One day as they prayed, there was a noise from the sky that sounded like a strong wind blowing, and it filled the whole house. Then they saw what looked like tongues of fire spreading out, and each person there was touched by a tongue. They were all filled with the Holy Spirit.
All	Help us to believe that you are with us, Jesus.
Reader Three	Some of the early followers tried to understand this great mystery. How does the Holy Spirit make Jesus present? St. John explains it this way: No one has ever seen God, but if we love one another God lives in us. Whoever declares that Jesus is the Son of God, God lives in that person. It is the Spirit who puts this faith in our hearts.
All	Help us to believe that you are with us, Jesus.

Reader Four	John goes on to say: This is the command that Jesus gives us, to love one another. When we do this, we are loving God. We can't say that Jesus is among us if we hate the people around us. When we love one another, our lives are in God and in Jesus. It is the Spirit who gives us the power to love.
All	Help us to believe that you are with us, Jesus.
Reader Five	Down through the ages, Christians have tried to understand how Jesus can be with us when we don't see him. We see signs of his presence and we feel it in our hearts, but we don't see him; we only see one another. People who have great faith understand that Jesus lives among us through others. How we treat others is how we treat Jesus.
All	Help us to believe that you are with us, Jesus.
Leader	Let us now talk to Jesus in the quiet of our hearts. Close your eyes and picture Jesus meeting you in the hall at school. Imagine how surprised you are. Is Jesus really at school with you? Walk down the hall with him and talk to him about anything that is on your mind.
	Allow two or three minutes for silent prayer.
Leader	Jesus, give us the gift of faith that we might believe in your presence among us. May we love and serve one another in your name. We ask these things…
All	In the name of the Father, and of the Son, and of the Holy Spirit. Amen.
Lenten Action	Invite children to discuss the words they repeated during this service: "Help us to believe that you are with us, Jesus." If Jesus is living in them and in those around them, how should they treat others? If they were to draw a picture of themselves reaching out to Jesus, how would they picture Jesus? Have each now do such a drawing. When all are completed, tape them together to form a mural.
	Now invite the children to stand around this mural and offer them these directions: "Look at the person next to you. Bow your head slightly in the direction of that person. He or she is a follower of Jesus, and Jesus dwells in that person."
	Encourage the children to bow inwardly before every person they meet the rest of this day and throughout the season of Lent.

6. Offering Peace

Introduction

Peace is not necessarily a concept that children understand. It's a word for grown-ups, and yet children, too, need the sense that God is with them, watching over them always. Explain to children that Jesus promised us the gift of peace at the Last Supper.

To Prepare

Place on your prayer table a votive candle, a Bible (open to John 14:27), and slips of paper (one for each child) with the names of countries or cities around the world where children are in danger because of war and violence.

Leader	Jesus, our risen savior, please teach us to offer others peace this Lent. We need your help to be peaceful people who offer only good things to those we meet in our daily lives. Please forgive us for the times we have made life difficult for others.
All	May the peace of Christ be in our hearts this Lent and always.
Reader One	Just as Jesus said to his followers at the Last Supper, "My peace I leave you; my peace I give to you," may each of us be bearers of peace this day.
All	May the peace of Christ be in our hearts this Lent and always.
Reader Two	Help us to be people of peace: at school and in religion class with classmates and teachers, and at home with our parents and brothers and sisters.
All	May the peace of Christ be in our hearts this Lent and always.
Leader	May there be peace in our hearts today and all through Lent. In silence, let us now talk to God in our own words about our need to share the good news that God is always with us.
	Pause for a moment of silent prayer.
Leader	Let there be peace on Earth, Holy Spirit, especially in countries torn by war and strife. Let there be peace in this country, in this parish, and in this class.
All	Amen.
Lenten Action	Give each child one of the slips of paper and have them take turns saying the place as all others respond, "May the children there live in peace." When all the places have been announced, have children offer one another a sign of peace. Encourage them to continue to pray throughout this lenten season for children who are not able to live in peace.

7. God Always Forgives

Introduction

As part of your lenten preparation, remind children often that they can offer reconciliation to others. They can offer one another peace and forgiveness anytime, anywhere. This service reminds them of the importance of saying they are sorry for their sins, not just during Lent, but in all the activities of their lives.

To Prepare

Place on your prayer table a bowl of holy water and a small sprig of evergreen, a votive candle, and a Bible (open to Acts of the Apostles 8:1–3; 9:3–6).

Leader	We gather together as God's children. Let us remember this Lent that God is full of gentleness and compassion for us. God knows us as we are, our good points and our weak ones. God strengthens us to do good, but also forgives us when we fail.
Reader One	For the times that we forget that we are brothers and sisters who should respect one another and help one another, Lord, have mercy.
All	Lord, have mercy.
Reader Two	For the times that we act selfishly, putting our own concerns before those of others, Christ, have mercy.
All	Christ, have mercy.
Reader Three	For the times we have hurt one another with our angry words or actions, Lord, have mercy.
All	Lord, have mercy.
Leader	No matter what we have done, Jesus offers us the chance to try again. Saint Paul, one of his early followers, was responsible for the deaths of many Christians before he had a change of heart. Listen to what the Bible says about Paul, who was first known by the name Saul.
Reader Four	Saul approved of the murder of Stephen the deacon, and he tried to destroy the church. He went from house to house where Christians lived and dragged the believers out, both men and women, and threw them into jail.
Leader	Jesus forgave Paul's stubborn pride and his hatred and gave him another chance. Listen now to how Jesus converted Paul.

61

Reader Five	On his way to Damascus, as Paul got near to the city, a light from the sky suddenly flashed all around him. He fell to the ground and heard a voice saying to him: "Saul, Saul! Why do you persecute me?" "Who are you, Lord?" he asked. "I am Jesus, the one you persecute," the voice said. Saul got up from the ground and opened his eyes, but he could not see a thing. He was blind.
Reader Six	After several days, God told Ananias, a holy man in Damascus, to cure Paul's blindness and to baptize him. Ananias said to Paul: "Jesus himself sent me, the one whom you saw on the road as you were coming here. He sent me so that you might see again and be filled with the Holy Spirit. " After that Paul became one of the most faithful and energetic of Jesus' followers. *The Word of the Lord.*
All	Thanks be to God.
Leader	If Jesus could forgive Paul's sins, he certainly will forgive ours. Let us now talk to Jesus about our need for his love and forgiveness this Lent. Close your eyes and picture Jesus sitting in your living room at home. Go sit beside him and talk to him about anything on your mind right now. Ask him to forgive you for any wrong you may have done this day.
	Allow two or three minutes for silent prayer.
Leader	Let us now resolve to love and forgive one another, as Jesus forgave Paul. Let us offer one another this greeting: The peace of Christ be with you. Response: And also with you.
Lenten Action	Before the children leave, invite them to stand in a circle around your prayer table. Ask one child to carry the bowl of water as you hold the sprig of evergreen. Move from child to child and lightly sprinkle each with the holy water. As you do so, say the following blessing: "(Child's name), let this water remind you to forgive others as Jesus forgives you."

8. Going Forward with Jesus

Introduction

This service reminds children that Jesus is with us always, not just during Lent, not just on Easter Sunday. This is one of the greatest teachings of our faith and one of the least practiced. "Remembering Jesus," then, is one of the best lenten practices children can embrace.

To Prepare

Place on your prayer table a Bible (open to John 15:18–19), a votive candle, and any symbol of Jesus you might have (a crucifix, a picture, or even something as simple as the name Jesus printed and decorated on a poster). Open this service in your regular class setting and process to your prayer table after the opening prayer below.

Leader	As we move forward on our lenten journey, one of our great joys is that Jesus moves forward with us. At the Last Supper he told us that he will not leave us alone—ever. May our belief in the presence of Jesus strengthen us to do the right thing today and all through Lent.
	Have one child hold high the symbol of Jesus as you process to your prayer area. Place the symbol on your prayer table as you pray the following loudly and dramatically.
Leader	Jesus, we believe that you give us life. Be with us always.

All	Jesus, we believe that you give us life. Be with us always.
Reader One	At the Last Supper, Jesus said to his followers: "I will not leave you orphans; I will come back to you. In just a little while the world will see me no more, but you will see me as one who has life, and you, too, will have life." *The Gospel of the Lord.*
All	Praise to you, Lord Jesus Christ.
Reader Two	If we feel sad or afraid today, Jesus, or if someone does something to hurt us, help us to remember that you are with us.
All	Jesus, we believe that you give us life. Be with us always.
Reader Three	When we are at prayer, or doing homework or chores, and when we are playing and relaxing, you are always with us.
All	Jesus, we believe that you give us life. Be with us always.
Leader	Every time we go to Mass, we hear the words, "The Lord be with you," and we answer, "and also with you." Let us ask God now in the quiet of our hearts to help us to believe these words and to truly live them as we await the resurrection of Christ at Easter.
	Pause for a moment of silent prayer.
Leader	Be with us, Jesus, our savior. Help us, strengthen us, and give us joy in your presence. Blessed are you who come in the name of the Lord.
All	Blessed are you, Jesus, this Lent and always. Amen.
Lenten Action	Begin today the practice of blessing the children as they leave your class with the words, "The Lord go with you," or a variation like "May Jesus walk with you today." Encourage them to offer a similar blessing to family members at home.

9. Loving One Another

Introduction

This service focuses on the many gifts God has given us and in particular the gift of love. Children may be focusing more on material gifts like new clothes, jewelry, CDs, videos, etc. than on all the spiritual gifts God has given them. This service invites them to pause and reflect on this.

To Prepare

Make small cards, one for each child, that say: "Live on in my love; Love one another." Place these in a container on your prayer table (a basket or bowl) as well as a Bible (open to John 15:9,17), and a votive candle.

Leader	God has given us many blessings. We have our families and friends. We have toys and games. We have our homes and our belongings. We have gifts of nature like sunshine and blue skies, rainbows and snow. Best of all, we have God's love for us, which no one can ever take away. One of the best ways to show our gratitude is to thank God often and to share our love with others.
All	May we live in your love, Jesus our brother.
Reader One	Jesus shared a great secret with his followers at the Last Supper. Here is what he said: "As the Father has loved me, so I have loved you. Live in my love…. The command I give you is this, that you love one another." *The Gospel of the Lord.*
All	Praise to you, Lord Jesus Christ.
Reader Two	Thank you, dear God, for giving us many good things in our lives. Thank you for every member of this class. May we share love and friendship this Lent and always.
All	May we live in your love, Jesus our savior.
Reader Three	Forgive us, loving God, for the times we forget how much you love us. Forgive us when we forget to love and care for others. Help us to change and grow as we make this journey through Lent.
All	May we live in your love, Jesus our redeemer.
Leader	Lent reminds us of God's great and generous love for us. Lent reminds us, too, that God is with us always. Let us each thank God in our own words now for this great gift of love.

Pause for a moment of silent prayer.

Leader   Thank you for Jesus and for all our gifts, loving God. Help us to be your true followers, this Lent and always, by loving others. We ask this in Jesus' name.

All   Amen.

Lenten Action   Explain to your children that love is a gift they can share anytime, anywhere. Encourage them to notice other children who need a kind word, a smile, or help with a difficult task, and then freely to give what they have been given. Before children leave your class, remind them of how much they are loved by God by distributing the cards you have prepared. Call children forward one by one and as you present the card, say: "Remember to love others this Lent and always."

10. Healing Our Hurts

Introduction

This service deals with the everyday conflicts children experience in their relationships with others. Childhood is filled with such conflicts. It is important therefore to remind children of their Christian call to deal with others fairly, to get along, and to build one another up—in spite of obstacles. One of the best practices for Lent is to show love and care to others.

To Prepare

Have available paper, pencils, and a container for the Lenten Action. Place on your prayer table a Bible (open to 1 John 4:20–21), a votive candle, and the container.

Leader	God, our heavenly parent, you know each of us by name and you love us in a very special way. Teach us how to imitate your love in our relationships with others. Even when it's hard, help us to offer love to others. We ask this in the name of Jesus, your son and our brother.
All	Amen.
Leader	Even when others hurt us, loving God, you ask us to return kindness for unkind words and to return good for evil. When we show love for others, we are also showing our love for you. Let us listen now to hear what God's Word says about this.
Reader One	In his letter to the early Christians, St. John wrote: "When people say that they love God, yet hate others, they are liars. Those who have no love for those they can see, cannot possibly love God whom they cannot see. The command we have from God is this: those who love God must also love other people." *The Word of the Lord.*
All	Thanks be to God.
Reader Two	God hears us whenever we ask for something. If someone hurts us, we should ask God to help us deal with that person lovingly, and God will answer our prayer. We belong to God, just as Jesus did, and Jesus will help us deal with the difficult people in our lives.
All	The commandment we have from God is this: those who love God must also love other people.
Reader Three	Give us courage, Jesus, when others make fun of us, leave us out of games, or even curse at us. Help us to practice love and forgiveness no matter how hard it is.

All	The commandment we have from God is this: those who love God must also love other people.
Reader Three	Sometimes it's very hard to love others, Jesus. When our friends betray us, or make us mad, or ignore us when someone more important to them is around, help us to practice love and forgiveness.
All	The commandment we have from God is this: those who really love God also love other people.
Leader	Think of someone in your life right now who is hurting you and making you unhappy. Picture this person clearly and then in your own words tell Jesus about him or her. Share exactly how you feel. (Pause for one minute.) Now ask Jesus to bless this person and to put love in his or her heart. (Pause.) Ask Jesus to also bless and heal you, so that your anger and hurt feelings will fade away.
	Pause for a moment of silent prayer.
Leader	God, our loving parent, help us to believe that you can change hearts. Help us, too, to offer love to others whenever we can during this lenten season. We ask these things in the name of Jesus, your son.
All	Amen.
Lenten Action	Give each participant a slip of paper and a pencil. After time for reflection, ask each to put on the slip the name of someone who is hurting them right now and then fold the slip so it can't be read by anyone else. Collect the slips and place them in a container. Have one of the children hold the container high as you say: "Help us to forgive those who hurt us, Jesus, this Lent and always." Leave these slips on your prayer table throughout Lent as a reminder to children to pray for the courage to forgive those who hurt them.

11. Praying Always

Introduction

This service emphasizes the importance of prayer, a traditional lenten practice, but also one that children can and should practice all year long. It also focuses on thanksgiving as a way of prayer. Its message is that there is more to prayer than "asking."

To Prepare

Make small scrolls, one for each child, with these messages on them: •The Lord is near •Present your needs to God •Pray prayers of thanksgiving •Let God's peace be in your heart •God hears our prayers •Let us trust in God always •Jesus is among us •May we praise God this day •Do not worry, trust God •Peace be with you •May we pray always •Guide us, loving God •Forgive us when we fail. If you have a large class, use the messages more than once. Place on your prayer table a Bible (open to Philippians 4:6–7), a container for the scrolls, and a votive candle.

Leader	Let us pray. We often ask you, loving God, for your help and guidance. This Lent, help us to ask with hearts full of gratitude, knowing that you hear our prayers and always do what is best for us. Let us listen now to what the Bible says about prayer.
Reader One	The Lord is near. Dismiss all anxiety from your minds. Present your needs to God in every form of prayer and in petitions full of gratitude. Then God's peace, which is beyond all understanding, will be in your hearts. *The Word of the Lord.*
All	Thanks be to God.
Reader Two	Give us the faith to believe that you hear us, great God, and remind us often through the day to turn our minds and hearts to you.
All	May all that we do this day be a prayer of praise and thanksgiving.
Reader Three	Teach us, too, gracious God, to pray for others: those who are sick, those who are lonely or sad, those who are poor and hungry. Help us to pray for those who can not or will not pray.
All	May all that we do this day be a prayer of praise and thanksgiving.
Leader	If we ask, God will help us to make all that we do a prayer. Sometimes our prayers will be for ourselves and others, sometimes they will be prayers of praise, and sometimes they will be prayers of sorrow. In silence, let us now pray to God in whatever way we want or need most.

Pause for a moment of silent prayer.

Leader   This Lent, may we be people of prayer who recognize that Jesus is among us always. Let us pray together…

All   Glory be to the Father, and to the Son,
and to the Holy Spirit,
as it was in the beginning, is now,
and ever shall be, world without end. Amen.

Lenten Action   Ask the children to stand in a circle. Carry the container and present it to each child, inviting him or her to take one of the scrolls. When everyone has a scroll, invite children to take turns reading (clearly and dramatically) what it says. Invite children to take these home to share with family members and as a reminder to say brief prayers of praise and thanks throughout Lent.

12. Listening to Jesus

Introduction

This service emphasizes the importance of quiet listening in prayer. Suggest to children that they might give up noise occasionally during Lent, so that they can think about the presence of Jesus and speak to him in the silence of their hearts.

To Prepare

If possible have available a small object, one for each child, that will serve as a reminder to be still and pray during Lent. For example, the objects might be: small seashells, small smooth stones, crosses made from twigs, or crosses cut from cardboard. Place these on your prayer table with a Bible (open to Mark 9:2–10), and a votive candle.

Leader	Holy Spirit, you are with us always. Help us to learn from you how to listen to one another and how to listen in the quiet of prayer to whatever words Jesus wants to speak to us.
All	May we always hear your Word within our hearts, dear Jesus.
Reader One	In one of the lenten gospels, we hear that Jesus went up a mountain with Peter, James, and John, and there his appearance became dazzling white. St. Mark says: "While the disciples were still marveling at what they had seen, a cloud came, covering them over, and out of the cloud a voice said, 'This is my son, my beloved son. Listen to him.'" *The Gospel of the Lord.*
All	Praise to you, Lord Jesus Christ.
Reader Two	Forgive us when we have been too busy with our own interests to really hear what family members, friends, and classmates are saying. Forgive us when we have been too busy to listen to you, our savior.
All	May we always hear your Word within our hearts.
Reader Three	Teach us, Jesus, our savior, how to open our minds and hearts to your guidance and help. Teach us how to listen to you.
All	May we always hear your Word within our hearts.
Leader	Holy Spirit, bless and watch over this class. Help us to love and respect one another and to show this by how we listen. Let us now close our eyes and be still as we listen to Jesus in the silence of our hearts.

Pause for a moment of silent prayer.

Leader   As we await your resurrection, Jesus, may we be open to the many ways that you speak to us in our daily lives. We ask this of God in your holy name.

All   Amen.

Lenten Action   Before children leave, invite them to come forward, one by one, to receive one of the objects you have prepared. As they come forward, make the sign of the cross on each forehead and then have them take a "sign of silence" from the prayer table.

Note: Make a special effort to invite children to practice the prayer of quiet during your lenten classes. Have them close their eyes as they pray. During each class slightly lengthen the time you spend in quiet prayer. Also encourage children to listen to what Jesus is saying to them through others, especially at home.

Optional Activity   Play "Bible Detective" by dividing the class into small groups of three or four. Give each group a Bible and challenge them to find as many examples of prayer (people praying, references to prayer gatherings, words of prayer, etc.) as they can. Allow ten minutes for this. When you call time, have the groups share what they have found.

13. Sharing Our Light

Introduction

Almsgiving is one of the traditional practices of Lent and even children can practice it. There are many ways that they can share what they have with others besides giving money. In particular they can share their Christian beliefs through good example. This service reminds them that they have many spiritual gifts and talents to share.

To Prepare

Place on your prayer table a Bible (open to Matthew 5:14–16), a votive candle, and a sign or poster that reads: "Jesus is the Light of the World." Have available pencils and index cards, one for each child, and a container to hold these.

Leader	God, Our Father, thank you for sending Jesus to guide and teach us. Help us, please, to follow him faithfully. He gave us so much; may we also share generously our gifts and talents with others this Lent. May we imitate Jesus, our light and our guide.
All	May we be faithful followers of Jesus, the light of the world.
Reader One	Jesus said to his friends and followers, "You are the light of the world. A city set on a hill cannot be hidden. People do not light a lamp and then put it under a bushel basket. They set it on a stand where it gives light to all in the house. In the same way, your light must shine before all so that they may see the goodness in your actions and praise your heavenly Father." *The Gospel of the Lord.*
All	Praise to you, Lord Jesus Christ.
Reader Two	May we share our light generously with others this Lent: with family members, with teachers and classmates, with friends and neighbors, and with everyone we meet.
All	May we be faithful followers of Jesus, the light of the world.
Reader Three	May we be generous, too, with those in our world who live in poverty. Help us to find ways to share the good things in our lives with them, and to at least share our concern by praying for them.
All	May we be faithful followers of Jesus, the light of the world.
Leader	God, Our Father, show us the way to Jesus. Help us to be generous this Lent in our love for others and through our good example. Help us to gladly share our time, our talents, and our prayers with others. Let us now pray

in silence for the gift to give of ourselves as generously as we can.

Pause for a moment of silent prayer.

Leader   Jesus, please help us to be generous—as you were. May your light shine through us so that others may believe in you. Together we pray…

All   Jesus, light of the world, pray for us.
Christ, light of the world, pray for us.
Jesus Christ, light of the world,
pray for us this Lent and always. Amen.

Lenten Action   Give each child one of the index cards and have each print on it one thing that he or she will try to do for someone else in the class this week. For example: I will smile at someone I don't like; I will pray for someone each night; I will invite someone to play at recess, etc. The children should not put their names on these cards.

When all have written a gift they can share, have them come forward one at a time to place their cards in the container on your prayer table. Remind them throughout Lent of their intention to offer someone in the class the light of Christ.

14. Living the Gospel

Introduction

This service focuses on our Christian call to imitate Jesus, especially through our joy, our patience, our thanksgiving, and our acceptance of God's forgiveness. It reminds children that Christians are called to do good and happy things as well as difficult and painful ones.

To Prepare

Have available popsicle sticks, one for each child, pieces of construction paper, scissors, and glue. If possible, also have several flower patterns that children can trace and cut out. (If time is a problem, precut the flowers). Place on your prayer table a Bible (open to Philippians 4:4–7) and a votive candle.

Leader	God of all seasons, God of light and darkness, guide us this Lent as we think about our call to follow Jesus and to live the message of the gospel. Help us to tell others of Jesus' presence in all that we say and do. We ask this in Jesus' name.
All	Amen.
Reader One	In the gospel Jesus tells us that whatever our sins, our faults and failings, God offers us forgiveness. And God offers us new life every day.
Reader Two	We believe in God's forgiveness, but we also know that we must change and grow, to become more like Jesus in our thinking and our actions.
Reader Three	Believing in Jesus means living his gospel message every day of our lives.
Reader Four	And so, knowing that Jesus is here with us, let us celebrate God's forgiveness, and try anew to change and grow.
Leader	God, our God, you are always forgiving. You love us more than we will ever know. Give us the courage this Lent to face our sins and to move away from them into your loving arms.
Reader Five	A reading from St. Paul's letter to the Philippians: (to be read slowly and dramatically) Rejoice in the Lord always, again I say rejoice! Let everyone see your patience. The Lord is near. Do not be afraid. Offer prayers of thanksgiving and tell God all your needs. And may God's amazing peace guard your hearts and minds in Christ Jesus. *The Word of the Lord.*

All	Thanks be to God.
Leader	I invite you now to close your eyes and listen…
	•Do you try to give joy to others? To your parents, sisters and brothers, friends, classmates, and teachers? Or do you more often make them sad by your actions?
	•Do you try to be patient, even when others make you wait? Are you polite even when you feel like getting mad?
	•Do you thank God often for all the gifts and talents you have received? Do you thank God for your family, your home, your education, your toys and belongings?
	•Do you pray for yourself and others, knowing that God listens with love? Do you pray for those in our world who are hurting from hunger, war, loneliness, or sadness of any kind?
	Allow time for children to reflect in silence.
Leader	Jesus, here with us, forgive us for all the things we do that hurt others. Forgive us for the times that we forget you are with us. Help us to be people of joy, patience, thanksgiving, and forgiveness, help us to be your true followers. We ask this…
All	…In the name of the Father and of the Son and of the Holy Spirit. Amen.
Lenten Action	Give each child a popsicle stick and a piece of construction paper. Have them draw or trace a flower shape and cut it out. Then ask them to print on the flower their name and one quality they would like to practice this Lent as a follower of Jesus, for example: joy, patience, thanksgiving, prayer, praise, forgiveness, etc. Then have them paste the flower to the popsicle stick. Arrange these on a piece of posterboard on which these words are written: Our lenten garden. Keep this in a visible place throughout Lent to remind children of the good qualities they have resolved to practice.

15. Learning to Be Gentle

Introduction

We often tell children that they are to follow Jesus, but we don't necessarily tell them how. This service emphasizes the gentleness of Jesus, a very important quality for children in their dealings with siblings and classmates. Thus, one answer about how to follow Jesus is: Be gentle and kind with your family members, friends, classmates, and teachers.

To Prepare

Place on your prayer table a Bible (open to Matthew 11:28–29), a votive candle, and a container with slips of paper on which these words are written: "Be gentle and kind to this person today." On the opposite side, print the name of a child in your class. Be sure that every child is named on one of the slips.

Leader	During Lent we are called to follow Jesus, but we sometimes forget that one way to follow him is to treat others with gentleness. Jesus called himself gentle and humble of heart, and he calls us to be the same.
All	May we be gentle and loving in all that we do this day.
Reader One	In St. Matthew's Gospel, Jesus speaks these words: "Come to me all you who are weary and find life difficult, and I will give you rest. Take my yoke upon you and learn from me, for I am gentle and humble of heart." *The Gospel of the Lord.*
All	Praise to you, Lord Jesus Christ.
Reader Two	Help us, Jesus our savior, to be gentle today with our toys, our games, our school books, our clothes, our home, and all our possessions.
All	May we be gentle and loving in all that we do this day.
Reader Three	Help us, Holy Spirit, to be gentle today with our friends, our teachers, our classmates, and everyone else we meet.
All	May we be gentle and loving in all that we do this day.

Leader	Help us, most of all, God our Father, to be gentle and loving with one another. Speak to us now in the quiet of our hearts about how to follow Jesus in the way of gentleness.
	Pause for a moment of silent prayer.
Leader	May we always go to Jesus when we have problems and difficulties. May we learn from him how to be gentle and humble of heart. Let us pray…
All	Jesus, meek and humble of heart, make our hearts like yours. Amen.
Lenten Action	Encourage children to regard all others as children of God. Ask them to make a special effort today to be gentle with someone who is unpopular and often left out. Have each child choose a name slip from the container on the prayer table and to follow its direction (without sharing whose name they have drawn). Encourage them to also pray for this person throughout Lent.
Optional Activity	Because some children go through their school years feeling left out or ridiculed by classmates, make a special effort this Lent to watch your class for any signs of such unkindness. If this is evident in your group (and even if it isn't) try playing "What If…" with your class.

Have children take turns drawing one of the following scenarios and sharing with the class what their response to it might be:
•What if your best friend begins to ignore you…
•What if other children call you names…
•What if your teacher isn't being fair…
•What if other kids make fun of your clothes…
•What if you notice that one child is always chosen last…
•What if you are always chosen last…
•What if no one will sit with you on the bus…
•What if other children always ignore you at recess…

Add any other scenarios that might apply to your group. The point is, do whatever you can this Lent to help children learn to be gentle with one another.

16. Walking with Jesus

Introduction

This service focuses on several lenten themes: the importance of daily prayer, thinking of others, and expressing our faith freely and often. In particular it emphasizes the necessity of being quiet and open to God's voice and direction.

To Prepare

Make copies of the following "Guidelines for Quiet Prayer," one for each child. 1. Find a quiet place where you will not be disturbed. 2. Get in a comfortable position and breathe in and out deeply five times. 3. As you breathe in, say to yourself: "Come, Holy Spirit," and as you breathe out say: "Go away worries and fears." 4. Say your favorite prayer slowly two times. 5. Sit quietly for at least a minute with your hands held open on your lap.

On your prayer table place a Bible (open to Matthew 18:19–20), a votive candle, and copies of the Guidelines.

Leader	May the grace of our Lord Jesus Christ, the love of God, and the fellowship of the Holy Spirit be with you all.
All	And also with you.
Leader	Loving God, Father, Son, and Holy Spirit, teach us to pray with the kind of faith you expect of us. Teach us to be silent at times that we might hear your answer to our prayers.
All	Our Father in Heaven, teach us how to pray.
Reader One	In the Gospel of St. Matthew, Jesus says this: "I tell you, if two of you join your voices on earth to pray for anything whatever, it shall be granted to you by my father in heaven. Whenever two or three of you gather in my name, I am there in your midst." *The Gospel of the Lord.*
All	Praise to you, Lord Jesus Christ.
Reader Two	Be with us as we pray our morning prayers and be with us at every hour of the day. Be with us as we close our day with prayer.
All	Jesus, our savior, teach us how to pray.
Reader Three	Help us to pray often for those in need, for peace in our world, for guidance for our church and national leaders, and for all those for whom we have promised to pray.
All	Holy Spirit, our helper and guide, teach us how to pray.

Leader	We need your help, our God, to learn the way of prayer. We are so used to noise that quiet prayer seems strange. Guide us now as we try to listen silently to you in our prayer.
	Pause for a moment of silent prayer.
Leader	You speak to us often, loving God, if only we would listen. Teach us how to pray—this Lent and always.
All	Father, Son, and Holy Spirit, teach us how to pray. Amen.
Lenten Action	Give each child a copy of the "Guidelines for Quiet Prayer" and read them over together. Then have children practice praying with the guidelines as you read them aloud (slowly and clearly). Invite children to take them home and share them with parents and siblings. Encourage them to pray this way at least once every day during the rest of Lent.

17. Carrying Our Crosses

Introduction

Use this service anytime during the six weeks of Lent. You might want to use the paper cross described below as a focal point for all your lenten prayers.

To Prepare

In or near your prayer space hang a large drawing of a cross, beneath which these words are written: "We Want to Follow Jesus." Have small slips of paper and pencils for each participant as well as a roll of tape. Also have available brown construction paper and scissors or pre-made small crosses, one for each child. Place on your prayer table a Bible (open to Luke 23:44–47) and a votive candle.

Leader	Glory and praise to you, Lord Jesus Christ. We greet you with love, and we ask that you help us listen carefully to your words.
All	Glory and praise to you, Lord Jesus Christ.
Leader	Lent is a six-week period when the whole church focuses on events in the life of Jesus. During these weeks we are invited to think about things that Jesus said and did. We move together during Lent toward Good Friday, the day that Jesus died on the cross, and we move from there to Easter Sunday and beyond, where we experience Jesus as our risen savior.
Reader One	During Lent, with our eyes on Jesus, we try to spend more time at prayer, more time talking to God and listening to God.
Reader Two	During Lent, with our eyes on Jesus, we try to be more aware of the needs of others, and to share our time and our money with the poor, the hungry, and the homeless.
Reader Three	During Lent, with our eyes on Jesus, we try to grow stronger by learning to say no to our sins and our failings, and by sometimes even saying no to the things we enjoy.
Leader	With our eyes on Jesus, we journey through Lent trying to understand and accept what God has in store for us. Jesus did this, and he is our example. Even as he died, Jesus gave himself over to whatever God wanted of him. Let us listen now to a description of his death on the cross:
Reader Four	It was about noontime, but darkness (like that from an eclipse of the sun) had settled over the whole land. This lasted until mid-afternoon. Jesus, having been on the cross three hours, uttered a loud cry and said: "Father,

into your hands I give over my spirit." After he said this, he died. Upon seeing what had happened, a soldier gave glory to God and cried out: "Surely this was an innocent man." *The Gospel of the Lord.*

All Praise to you, Lord Jesus Christ.

Leader Let us now reflect for a few moments about what we have just heard. Close your eyes and speak to Jesus in your own words about the things that happened to him. Talk to him, too, about things that are happening in your life.

Allow two to three minutes of silence for this.

Leader I will now distribute small slips of paper on which you can write a word or two to describe how you will try to become a better person this Lent. We will attach these to the paper cross on our prayer table and display it.

Allow time for writing and then have participants come forward one at a time to attach their papers to the cross. When all have attached their papers, have two children hold up the cross for the closing prayer.

Leader Jesus, please receive our good intentions. Help us to be true to them through all of Lent. We adore you, O Christ, and we praise you.

All Because by your holy cross you have redeemed the world.

Lenten Action If you have time, let children to make small paper crosses to take home as a reminder that Jesus is always with them. Or give out the pre-made crosses. Invite children to put their names on one side of the cross and the name "Jesus" on the other.

18. Forgiving One Another

Introduction

Children may not realize how often they have opportunities to forgive others. Before you begin this prayer service, ask them to think of situations when forgiveness is called for. Do they offer it? Are there times when they can offer forgiveness to their parents and/or siblings, to playmates, even to friends who hurt them in some way?

To Prepare

Cut out strips of colored paper, 1" x 8", one for each child, and have available pencils and tape. Choose three or four children and explain to them privately that at the end of the service you will be demonstrating what happens when we do not forgive others. They will be your "unforgiven" ones. On your prayer table place a Bible (open to Colossians 3:13) and a votive candle.

Leader	Blessed are you, loving God, and blessed is everything you have made. We praise you and we thank you. Glory be to the Father and to the Son and to the Holy Spirit…
All	…As it was in the beginning, is now, and ever shall be, world without end. Amen.
Leader	In this time of Lent, we are moving toward Easter, remembering that Jesus loves and forgives us, no matter what. We pray that God will help us to imitate Jesus with patience and love.
All	May we be patient with one another, always ready to forgive.
Reader One	In his letter to the Christians in Colossae, St. Paul wrote: "Accept life and be patient with one another; forgive as freely as the Lord has forgiven you." *The Word of the Lord.*
All	Thanks be to God.
Reader Two	As we prepare for Easter, may we keep Jesus in our minds and hearts. May we practice forgiveness in our dealings with friends, teachers, neighbors, and all others we meet.
All	May we be patient with one another, always ready to forgive.
Reader Three	During Lent, we are asked by the church to change and grow and to make sacrifices to reach this goal. But one of the best ways to grow is to have a forgiving heart.

All	May we be patient with one another, always ready to forgive.
Leader	As we now speak to God in the silence of our hearts, let us pray for the gift of forgiveness, and may God forgive us for the times we have been impatient with others.
	Pause for a moment of silent prayer.
Leader	Teach us forgiveness, Jesus our savior. As we walk this lenten journey, give us the courage to follow you. As you prayed for your enemies from the cross, so help us to pray for those who have hurt us. We ask this in your holy name…
All	Amen.
Lenten Action	Distribute the strips of paper and have each child write his or her name on the strip. Then invite children to hold their strips as they form a circle. Have the child on your right begin by asking you: Do you freely forgive me? If you answer yes, tape that child's strip inside yours to begin forming a chain. Go around the circle with each child asking you the same question.
	When you come to those you chose beforehand to be "unforgiven," however, you answer no, and they have to step back out of the circle. When all have had a turn, ask the children in the circle what you should do about those left out. (Ideally they will want you to forgive the unforgiven ones.) Once you have forgiven them, they will need to become part of the circle, so other children will have to untape their strips to let them in. Ask the left out ones how it felt to be unforgiven.
	Before the children leave, remind them to freely offer forgiveness to their families and others throughout the rest of Lent.

19. Sharing Living Water

Introduction

One of the Sunday lenten readings is about Jesus and the Samaritan "woman at the well." In the course of their conversation, Jesus offers her living water. This service focuses on that promise and what it means in the lives of children today.

To Prepare

On your prayer table, place a Bible (open to John 4:3), a votive candle, and a container of holy water (if available). Plain water will do.

Leader	Jesus gives us the gift of living water, water that makes us clean and fresh in God's sight. As followers of Jesus, we are called to offer others living water—the water of kindness and understanding, the water of patience and love—not just during Lent, but all year through.
All	Give us living water, Jesus, and wash our sins away.
Reader One	The Gospel of John tells the story of Jesus meeting the woman at the well. He said to her, "If only you could recognize God's gift and who it is that is asking you for a drink, you would have asked him instead to give you living water." *The Gospel of the Lord.*
All	Praise to you, Lord Jesus Christ.
Reader Two	Guide us today that we might share your living water with everyone in this class. May we share our faith and sing God's praises together.
All	Give us living water, Jesus, and wash our sins away.
Reader Three	Help us to share living water today with our family members, friends, neighbors, and with relatives and others who visit us.
All	Give us living water, Jesus, and wash our sins away.
Leader	Let us ask God to refresh us with the living water of faith. And let us talk to God in the silence of our hearts now that we might truly live the promises we made as we were washed in the waters of baptism.
	Pause for a moment of silent prayer.
Leader	Jesus, as you offered the woman at the well love and forgiveness, please give these gifts to us as well. We need your life-giving water in every way, this Lent and always. (Now hold up the container of water as you pray:)

"May this water remind us that Jesus is here with us, offering us his living water."

All Give us this living water, Jesus, and wash our sins away. Amen.

Lenten Action Place the container of water back on the prayer table and invite children to come forward one at a time for a blessing. As you sign each on the forehead (in a shape of a cross), say: "(Name of child), remember that Jesus gives living water." Invite children to respond "Amen." When the children have all received a blessing, invite one of them (or all of them) to give you a blessing as well.

20. Doing God's Will

Introduction

This service focuses on doing God's will, a concept foreign to many children (and adults) today. We know from Scripture that God's will is that we should love others as Jesus loves us. Thus, when we honor and respect all others, we are well on our way to doing God's will.

To Prepare

Print the following messages on small slips of paper (be sure there is one for each child. If your class is large, use the messages more than once): Do not make fun of anyone today; Smile at someone who is sad or lonely; Listen to your parents today; Show respect to your teachers today; Share with your brothers and sisters today; Remember to say prayers of thanks today; Play with someone who is left out today; Do not hurt anyone's feelings today; Say thank you often today.

On your prayer table place a Bible (open to John 14:15–16), a votive candle, and a basket or bowl for the messages.

Leader	Obedience is doing God's will to the best of our ability. God wants us to be good family members, good students, and good friends. Jesus was obedient and always tried to understand what God wanted him to do. May Jesus be our model this Lent and always.
All	Send us your Spirit, Lord, that we might obey your commands.
Reader One	At the Last Supper Jesus promised his followers that he would send them a helper, someone who would guide them and be with them always. Here's what he said. "Anything you ask me in my name I will do. If you love me and obey the commands I give you, I will ask the Father and he will give you the Spirit to be with you always." *The Gospel of the Lord.*
All	Praise to you, Lord Jesus Christ.
Reader Two	In imitation of Jesus, God asks us to share what we have with those in need and to be content with less rather than more. Help us, Jesus, to do God's will.
All	Send us your Spirit, Lord, that we might obey your commands.
Reader Three	In imitation of Jesus, God asks us to be content with what we have and to pray with grateful hearts, throughout this Lent and always.
All	Send us your Spirit, Lord, that we might obey your commands.
Leader	In this journey through Lent, Jesus reminds us that being his followers

demands that we obey God's will for us. In silence let us now ask God to help us to do this.

Pause for a moment of silent prayer.

Leader Help us to do your will, loving God, and to pray often for the strength and courage that only you can give. Thank you for all your gifts.

All Thank you for the gift of your Holy Spirit. Amen.

Lenten Action Ask children if they know what it means to do God's will. Explain that first and foremost it means loving and respecting one another, and we can do this in many simple ways throughout the day. Invite children to go up to the prayer table and take one of the slips of paper before they leave class. Each slip offers a suggestion for "doing God's will." Encourage children to practice these suggestions for the rest of the week.

21. Making Others Happy

Introduction

Though most people consider Lent a time to prepare for the resurrection of Jesus, it is actually a time to strengthen our belief in the resurrection. Jesus has been raised up, once and for all, and for this we can rejoice—even during Lent. Explain to children that one of the best practices for Lent is to give joy to others.

To Prepare

Beforehand make a prayer card for each child with this prayer on it: "Jesus, our risen savior, help us to give joy to others this Lent and always. Amen." On your prayer table place a Bible (open to Colossians 3:16), a votive candle, and a container for the prayer cards.

Leader	Many people think that Lent is a time for sadness. But it is actually also a time for joy and happiness. As Christians we rejoice most of all because Jesus has been raised from the dead. This is the good news we celebrate at Easter. Lent is our time to strengthen our belief in the resurrection.
All	May we praise God with joy and happiness for the gift of Jesus.
Reader One	In his letter to the Christians of Colossae, St. Paul wrote these words: "Teach and help one another with psalms and hymns and Christian songs, always singing God's praises with cheerful hearts." *The Word of the Lord.*
All	Thanks be to God.
Reader Two	Guide us this day, loving God, that we might give joy and cheer to others because of our faith in Jesus. Help us to rejoice even during Lent because Jesus is our savior and our friend.
All	May we praise God with joy and happiness for the gift of Jesus.
Reader Three	As we make sacrifices this Lent, share what we have with others, and pray together as a class, may we do so with great joy.
All	May we praise God with joy and happiness for the gift of Jesus.
Leader	We need God's help to prepare well for Easter, the feast of joy. Even during Lent, we can share our happiness with others. Let us talk to God in the silence of our hearts about ways we can help one another and everyone we meet, to be happy.

Pause for a moment of silent prayer.

Leader	Forgive us, loving God, for those times we have made others sad. Help us to see Jesus present in everyone we meet.
All	All praise and honor to you, Lord Jesus Christ, now and forevermore. Amen.
Lenten Action	Encourage children to pray often this Lent for the gift of happiness for people who are lonely, sad, or left out. Ask them to pray, too, for children throughout the world who are unhappy because of war or poverty. Before class ends, have children come forward, one by one, to receive a prayer card. Remind them to share this prayer with family members and to say it throughout Lent.

22. Doing the Right Thing

Introduction

This service encourages children to keep going with their lenten practices, especially the practice of loving others in imitation of Jesus. Six weeks is a long time for young people and they need at least weekly reminders from you to persevere.

To Prepare

Beforehand make a sign or poster (with children's help) that says "Do the Right Thing!" Place this on or near your prayer table. Also place there a Bible (open to 1 John 3:23) and a votive candle.

Leader	It is very hard to keep up our lenten practices of prayer, almsgiving (sharing), and fasting from things that are not good for us. Let us ask God today to give us new energy for doing the right thing. We learn in Scripture the source of this kind of energy.
Reader One	St. John wrote these encouraging words to the early Christians: "God's commandment is this: we should believe in the name of his son, Jesus Christ, and love one another just as he commanded us."
All	Help us to keep moving toward Easter, Jesus our brother.
Reader Two	May God's love guide us in all our dealings with others. May all who meet us recognize that we are God's beloved children who believe in the resurrection of Jesus and who do the right thing.
All	Help us to keep moving toward Easter, Jesus our savior.
Reader Three	May God help us to be strong in our faith, to give good example to others, and to say we are sorry when we fail.
All	Help us to keep moving toward Easter, Jesus our friend.
Leader	Let us renew our promise to prepare for Easter, believing that Jesus is here with us. Let us now talk to God in the silence of our hearts about our need for courage to do the right thing.
	Pause for a moment of silent prayer.
Leader	We await your resurrection, Jesus. Help us to keep moving forward with love and thanksgiving. All praise be to you, Lord Jesus Christ.
All	Now and forevermore. Amen.

Lenten Action   Ask the children what they think doing the right thing means in practical terms. Have one child record everyone's suggestions on slips of paper. (Have a few suggestions of your own written on slips, for example: Help your parents; respect your teachers; be polite to everyone; be kind to classmates (especially those who are left out); keep your room neat; do your homework carefully). Before the children leave have each choose one slip and encourage them to try throughout the week to practice what is on it.

23. Loving Our Enemies

Introduction

This service focuses on children's relationships with one another. They may not think that they have "enemies," so it might be important to explain that when they intentionally leave others out, or make fun of others, they are being the enemy. They are called to love without exception (as Jesus does). Children who are the victims of such behavior have to deal with forgiving their "enemies."

To Prepare

Place the names of the children in your class (on index cards) in a container. Place this on your prayer table as well as a Bible (open to Matthew 5:43) and a votive candle.

Leader	God, you are a loving and forgiving God. No matter what we do you welcome us with open arms. Help us to be the same toward those who have hurt us in any way. Help us to love them.
All	Teach us to love and forgive our enemies, Jesus our brother.
Reader One	In St. Matthew's Gospel, Jesus told the people, "Love your enemies; pray for those who harm you… try in every way to love everyone without exception, as God does." *The Gospel of the Lord.*
All	Praise to you, Lord Jesus Christ.
Reader Two	If other children make fun of us, call us names, or refuse to include us in their games…
All	Teach us to love and forgive our enemies, Jesus our savior.
Reader Three	If our parents have been unfair or if our friends have disagreed with us or told lies about us…
All	Teach us to love and forgive our enemies, Jesus our redeemer.
Leader	Jesus forgave those who crucified him. From the cross he prayed, "Father, forgive them; they don't know what they are doing." Let us ask God in silence to give us forgiving hearts that we might be true followers of Jesus.
	Pause for a moment of silent prayer.
Leader	Teach us to forgive, merciful God, this Lent and always. Help us to forgive one another, our family members, friends, and most of all our enemies.

All   Teach us to love and forgive our enemies, Jesus, this Lent and always. Amen.

Lenten Action Invite children to stand in a circle around your prayer table in silence. Move from one to the next with the container of index cards and have each child draw one out. When all have a card, instruct children to look at the name on it. Then ask them to fold their hands (with the card between their hands) and to close their eyes. Say the following:

"God our Father loves the person whose name you have drawn very much. God thinks very highly of this person. If you have been unkind to this person in any way, ask God to forgive you now. (pause) If this person has been unkind to you in any way, ask God to help you to forgive. (pause) Remember to pray for this person today and all through the week."

Before they leave have children drop the name back into the prayer table container.

24. Learning to Give "Alms"

Introduction

One of the central practices of Lent is almsgiving. Since children do not have much money (though some do), emphasize the many other ways that they can reach out to those in need. By giving others time and attention, smiles and reassurances, they are practicing almsgiving.

To Prepare

Have available pieces of construction paper (Easter colors, if possible), pencils, and markers. Place on your prayer table a Bible (open to Luke 6:36–38) and a votive candle.

Leader	Jesus, in Scripture you tell us that if we are generous with others, God will be very, very generous with us, so much so that our gifts will be overflowing. Help us to understand, however, that it is better to give than to receive.
All	Jesus, help us to share our time and attention with others this Lent.
Reader One	In St. Luke's Gospel, Jesus said to his followers, "Give, and it shall be given to you, pressed down, shaken together, running over…. If you give much, you will also receive much." *The Gospel of the Lord.*
All	Praise to you, Lord Jesus Christ.
Reader Two	We pray today, not just for ourselves, but for those who need food, clothing, shelter, medicine, heat for their homes, clean water, and so many other things that we take for granted.
All	Jesus, help us to share our gifts and talents with others this Lent.
Reader Two	If there is a child at school who needs a friend or a teacher who needs assistance, give us the courage to share our friendship, and the patience to share our time.
All	Jesus, help us to share our smiles and our friendship with others this Lent.
Leader	Jesus you know how difficult it is sometimes for us to share our time, our friendship, and our money. We would rather keep these things for ourselves. Guide us as we now think about ways that we can be generous to others—as God is generous to us.
	Pause for a moment of silent prayer.
Leader	Thank you, God, for all your gifts. Help us to share them generously with others this Lent and always. We ask this in Jesus' name…

All   Amen.

Lenten Action   Lent is a good time to reflect on our call to follow Jesus. In preparation for Easter, invite children to think about their name saint (or a favorite saint) and to compose a prayer to that saint for someone who needs a boost (a lonely neighbor, an elderly relative, a child who feels left out). A sample prayer might be:

"Saint Joseph, please pray for my neighbor Mrs. Carlyle. Ask Jesus to help her feel better. Amen." If possible, give the children pieces of construction paper for these prayers, and if you have time, encourage them to decorate them. Encourage them, too, to deliver these to the person they have prayed for sometime before Easter.

25. Healing Our Blindness

Introduction

In this service, children are encouraged to view blindness as more than physical. Just as Jesus cured the man born blind, he can cure them of their spiritual blindness. What is spiritual blindness? The refusal to see God's goodness reflected in all God's children. We all need to be healed.

To Prepare

Place in your prayer area a poster that reads: Jesus, heal our blindness. Place on your prayer table a Bible (open to John 9:1–41) and a votive candle.

Leader
Jesus, you once gave sight to a man born blind. You told him that you are the light of the world, and that seeing with faith is more important than seeing with the eyes. And yet you cured him. He was blind but then he could see.

All
Open our eyes and our hearts to your presence among us, Jesus.

Reader One
In many ways we are all blind, not in our eyes, but in our hearts. We don't see God's hand guiding us. In St. John's Gospel, Jesus said to his followers: "We must do the works of God while it is day. When the night comes on, no one can work. While I am in the world, I am the light of the world." *The Gospel of the Lord.*

All
Praise to you, Lord Jesus Christ.

Reader Two
We are blind, Jesus, in many ways. Though our eyes can see, we do not place our faith in you. We do not see that you are here with us, even though you have told us so.

All
Open our eyes and our hearts to your presence among us, Jesus.

Reader Three
We are sometimes blind to the needs of others. We look the other way

when someone is sad or lonely or left out. Cure our blindness, Jesus. Help us to see those in need and to respond.

All   Open our eyes and our hearts to your presence among us, Jesus.

Leader   We are children of the light, called to imitate Jesus, the light of the world. Let us ask God in the silence of our hearts to help us grow in faith that we might see the needs of others more clearly.

Pause for a moment of silent prayer.

Leader   Thank you, God, for giving us Jesus. Just as he cured the man born blind, may he cure our blindness too.

All   Open our eyes and our hearts to your presence among us, Jesus. Amen.

Lenten Action   If possible, darken your teaching space and leave the votive candle lit. Invite children to spend a longer time in silent prayer, asking Jesus, the light of the world, to guide them as they prepare for his resurrection at Easter.

Encourage them to ask their parents to light a candle at dinnertime throughout the rest of Lent as a reminder that Jesus is always with them.

26. Serving Others First

Introduction

Giving service can be a vague and unfamiliar concept for children, so it is necessary to help them to see practical ways to serve. Reaching out to a needy child is a way to serve that child's need for friendship and inclusion. Helping parents or teachers carry their "burdens" is a way to serve them. Emphasize to children the importance of offering daily service to others throughout the lenten season. This is one of the best ways to observe Lent.

To Prepare

Write out some "service" situations (as below under Lenten Action) and place these on your prayer table. Also place there a Bible (open to Matthew 23:1–12) and a votive candle.

Leader	One of the practices of Lent is service. We cannot serve others, however, if we think we are better than they are. Jesus teaches us that we are all equal in God's eyes.
All	God, our loving parent, hear our prayer. Help us to serve others with love and care.
Reader One	In St. Matthew's Gospel, Jesus tells his followers, "Do not imitate those who do good only to be praised by others. And do not always choose first place. The greatest among you is the one who serves the rest." *The Gospel of the Lord.*
All	Praise to you, Lord Jesus Christ.
Reader Two	Help us, dear God, to serve anyone who is in need: old, young, brown, white, male, female, friend, stranger, rich, or poor.
All	God, our loving parent, hear our prayer. Help us to serve others with love and care.
Reader Three	Help us to serve those who are lonely or afraid, hungry or cold, sick or neglected. May we serve all others in Jesus' name.
All	God, our loving parent, hear our prayer. Help us to serve others with love and care.
Leader	It takes courage to serve those who can give us nothing in return. Let us ask God for this courage as we now pray in silence.
	Pause for a moment of silent prayer.

Leader	Help us, Jesus, to be "great" in our love and service to others.
All	God, our loving parent, hear our prayer. Help us to serve others with love and care. Amen.
Lenten Action	Invite children to role-play some typical situations in which they might be called to share their time and attention with someone. Place several such situations in a container and have children form groups of three. Have each group draw out one of these situations and perform it for the rest of the class.

Sample situations might be as follows.
•Two children are talking about a movie they saw. A third child approaches and tries to join the conversation. One of the first two doesn't like this intruder and is rude to him or her. The other child, however, does extend friendship.
•A teacher is walking down the hall with a load of books as two children approach. One child suggests that they help the teacher; the other says no because that teacher was mean to him or her once. One helps the teacher and the other goes on by.
•Two children are asked to choose a third child to do a small group project with them. The only person left to choose, however, is an unpopular child. They want to do the project by themselves, but the teacher wants groups of three. What should they do?

Leave time afterward for children to discuss how they felt about these (and other situations you may have devised).

27. Learning to Say No

Introduction

Giving up simple pleasures is a traditional practice of Lent. But explain to children that we don't give up things for the sake of giving them up. We do so to help ourselves grow strong in the face of difficult choices. Encourage children to "just say no" this Lent to anything that leads them away from following Jesus. Ask them to suggest ways they might do this. Remind them to begin small. Another very important lenten practice for children is to be aware of the hurting ones among them: those who are different, left out, made fun of, disregarded, etc. Encourage them throughout Lent to actively reach out to others who are sad or lonely.

To Prepare

Prepare cards, one for each child, that have the words "Just Say No" on them. Place these on your prayer table in a container, and also place there a Bible (open to Matthew 10:38) and a votive candle.

Leader	God, our loving God, on this lenten journey, we need many gifts from you, like love, joy, generosity, and patience. But we also need help to say no to our bad habits, like anger, laziness, and impatience.
All	Make us strong, dear God. Help us say no to whatever is wrong.
Reader One	Jesus told his followers, "Those who do not take up their cross and come after me are not worthy of me. Those who seek only themselves bring themselves to ruin."
All	Make us strong, dear God. Help us say no to whatever is wrong.
Reader Two	We can only say no to our bad habits if we also say no in simpler ways. During Lent we can say no to sin, but also to foods that aren't good for us or TV programs that distract us from homework or chores.
All	Make us strong, dear God. Help us say no to whatever is wrong.
Reader Two	Saying no to ourselves can make us strong. Give us the courage this day, dear God, to say no when we are tempted to be mean to someone, or to skip our chores, or to be rude to one another.
All	Make us strong, dear God. Help us say no to whatever is wrong.
Leader	Let us ask God in the silence of our hearts to help us say yes today to listening to one another, sharing with one another, and being patient with one another.

Pause for a moment of silent prayer.

Leader Help us to say no to all that leads us from you, loving God. Make us strong this day and every day of Lent. We ask this in Jesus' name…

All Amen.

Lenten Action Invite children to close their eyes as you lead the following reflection:

"Jesus, what do you want us to say no to this day? What bad habits, unhealthy eating patterns, or behaviors toward others should we say no to?" Ask children to think of at least one thing that they need to say no to right now. Then distribute the cards and have them fill in that one thing.

Encourage them to try hard to follow through, not only on this day but for the rest of Lent.

28. Turning the Other Cheek

Introduction

This service focuses on forgiving when others have injured or insulted us. Name calling, exclusion, and taunting are typical childhood faults, and they can cause immense pain in the ones who are victimized by them. Encourage children to be more aware of the feelings of others, and encourage those who suffer hurt feelings to try to forgive.

To Prepare

Place on your prayer table a container (a bowl or basket) that hold blank slips of paper, pencils, a Bible (open to Matthew 5:38–39) and a candle.

Leader	God, in this lenten season of prayer and penance, help us to practice the greatest penance of all, loving and forgiving those who have hurt us. Jesus has shown us the way. Help us to imitate him.
All	Teach us, Holy Spirit, to follow Jesus, this Lent and always.
Reader One	In St. Matthew's Gospel, Jesus said to his followers, "You have heard the commandment: an eye for an eye, a tooth for a tooth. But what I say to you is this: 'Offer no resistance to injury. When a person strikes you on the right cheek, turn and offer the other cheek.'" *The Gospel of the Lord.*
All	Thanks be to God.
Reader Two	If our parents or brothers and sisters have made us angry or hurt our feelings, if our friends have neglected us in any way…
All	Teach us, Holy Spirit, to follow Jesus, this Lent and always.
Reader Three	If a teacher has been rude today, or if a friend has been unkind, if a classmate has been spiteful…
All	Teach us, Holy Spirit, to follow Jesus, this Lent and always.
Leader	Teach us how to turn the other cheek, loving God. Help us to forgive one another, our friends, and even our enemies. We ask you now in silence to show us the way.
	Pause for a moment of silent prayer.
Leader	It is so easy for us to hold grudges, to not want to forgive others for hurting us. This Lent, forgiving God, help us to turn the other cheek.

All   Teach us, Holy Spirit, how to follow Jesus, this Lent and always. Amen.

Lenten Action   Invite each child to come forward and take a slip of paper from the container. Ask each to write on this slip (in private) someone he or she finds hard to forgive. Have them fold these and place them back in the container. Lift this as you pray:

"Dear God, before we end this class, we ask you to help us forgive those whose names are here. Forgive us, too, if we have hurt others."

Afterward, discard the slips, and tell the children you will be doing so (without reading them).

29. Coming from the Tomb

Introduction

This service focuses on one of the most dramatic and moving stories in the Gospel of John. Jesus raises his close friend Lazarus from the dead. Explain to children that all of us will be raised up to new life through the power of Jesus. The story of Lazarus gives us hope.

To Prepare

Using posterboard, draw a large cross and place it on or near your prayer table. Also have available small pieces of paper for each child, pencils or pens, tape, a Bible (open to John 11:1–45) and a votive candle.

Leader	All during Lent, we are moving toward Easter when we will celebrate the resurrection of Jesus. Lent is also our time to prepare for being raised up. Just as Jesus called his friend Lazarus from the tomb, he calls us to new life.
All	Give us new life, Jesus, our risen savior, this Lent and always.
Reader One	Jesus said to his followers, "Did I not assure you that if you believed in me you would see the glory of God?" Then they took away the stone…and Jesus called out loudly, "Lazarus, come out!"
All	Give us new life, Jesus, our risen savior, this Lent and always.
Reader Two	You called yourself the resurrection and the life, Jesus. Help us to celebrate every day of our lives with joy and thanksgiving.
All	Give us new life, Jesus, our risen savior, this Lent and always.
Reader Three	Help us to be grateful for the wonderful gifts you give us: our family life, our home, our friends, our school, and our parish.
All	Give us new life, Jesus, our risen savior, this Lent and always.

Leader	Help us to believe as Lazarus and his sisters did, that you will raise us up from selfishness and greed to generosity and love. Show us the way, Jesus, as we now pray.
	Pause for a moment of silent prayer.
Leader	We believe that you are the resurrection and the life. We ask you please, Jesus, to call us forth as you called your friend, Lazarus.
All	You are the way, the truth, and the life for us, Jesus. Call us forth this Lent and always. Amen.
Lenten Action	In the story of the raising of Lazarus from the dead, it is written that Jesus wept at the tomb of his friend because he loved him so much. Invite children to write a four-line reflection about their reaction to the tears of Jesus. This can be a poem, a prayer, a statement, a question, etc.
	When all are written, attach them to the large paper cross on on near your prayer table.
Optional Activity	Divide children into groups of three and challenge each group to plan and then perform a role-play of the raising of Lazarus (John 11:1–45). They can choose any part of the story and they should try to present it in a contemporary manner. Allow ten minutes or so for the planning and then have children perform their role-play for the total group.

30. Remembering Jesus

Introduction

As a sign of his love and care, Jesus asked his followers at the Last Supper to break bread together and to share wine together in memory of him. We continue to do this today, every week at Mass. In this service children are invited to recall that Jesus is always with them, watching over them, aware of their worries and concerns.

To Prepare

Place on your prayer table a Bible (open to Luke 12:20–34), a plate of bread (a small piece for each participant), a jug of grape juice, small paper cups, one for each child, and a votive candle.

Leader	Blessed are you, Lord God of all creation. Through your goodness we have bread to offer, which earth has given and human hands have made. It will become for us the Bread of Life.
All	Blessed be God forever.
Leader	Blessed are you, Lord God of all creation. Through your goodness we have wine to offer, fruit of the vine and work of human hands. It will become our spiritual drink.
All	Blessed be God forever.
Leader	Blessed are you, Lord God, for you nourish us, too, with your Word. Open our hearts and minds as we now listen.
Reader One	A reading from the Gospel of Luke: Jesus said these words to the people: "I tell you, you shouldn't worry about life, wondering what you're going to eat or what you're going to wear. Think of the birds outside. They don't worry about these things, and yet God feeds them.
Reader Two	"And look at the flowers in the fields. They don't worry either, and yet they are more beautiful than a king's finest robes. When you put your mind on God and the things of God, everything else will be taken care of." *The Gospel of the Lord.*
All	Praise to you, Lord Jesus Christ.
Leader	Let us pray. God, we ask you to help us not to worry. Help us to believe that you will take care of us because you love us and guide us always. Please hear our prayers.

Reader Three	Help us not to worry about having snack foods and drinks, but rather to consider sharing our food and drink with those in need.
All	Teach us how to trust in you.
Reader Four	Help us not to worry about wearing expensive clothes, but rather to share our clothing with those who have far less than we do.
All	Teach us how to trust in you.
	Invite children to pray spontaneously about additional "worries" they may have. After these petitions, continue as follows.
Leader	Jesus, you know our worries and concerns. Watch over us and provide for us and help us to watch over and care for one another. Teach us how to trust in you.
All	Amen.
Lenten Action	Before children leave, encourage them to remember Jesus by saying the following: "Let us now share these gifts of bread and juice as a reminder of the presence of Jesus. May these gifts help us to remember that God takes care of us not only during Lent and Holy Week, but always."
	(Explain to the children that this sharing is only a symbol and reminder of what we do at Mass.)
	Pass each child a piece of bread and a cup of juice saying: "(Child's name), remember that God takes care of you."
	Conclude by inviting children to offer one another a sign of peace.

31. Singing Hosanna

Introduction

This service recalls Jesus' triumphal entry into Jerusalem (which is read on Palm Sunday (also called Passion Sunday). It helps children to understand that they, too, might be praising Jesus only when they are happy, but perhaps forget his presence when they are hurting in any way.

To Prepare

Have available Bibles that children can use for the "Lenten Action" below as well as paper and pencils. Place on your prayer table a Bible (open to Mark 11:1–10), a votive candle, and a palm branch, if available.

Leader	You entered Jerusalem, Jesus, the week before you died, and the people cheered you. They waved palm branches and shouted "Hosanna, praise to you, Jesus."
All	Blessed is he who comes in the name of the Lord. Hosanna in the highest.
Reader One	Many people spread their cloaks on the road and others spread leafy branches they had cut from the fields. Everyone was shouting, "Hosanna! Blessed is he who comes in the name of the Lord."
Reader Two	We say these words each week at Mass. Help us to live them by praying our thanks and praise every day of our lives.
All	We thank you and praise you, Jesus. Hosanna in the highest.
Reader Three	At the end of the week you were arrested, and people went from cries of praise to cries of hatred. "Crucify him," they said.
All	Forgive us for the times we have denied you, Jesus. Hosanna in the highest.
Leader	Jesus, it's easy to praise you when things go well for us. Help us to learn how to also praise you when things are difficult. We ask you now in silence to teach us to be people of praise, in good times and bad.
	Pause for a moment of silent prayer.
Leader	Teach us to praise you often at home, at school, and wherever we go.
All	Blessed is he who comes in the name of the Lord. Hosanna in the highest.

Lenten Action   Invite children to do a contemporary news story about Jesus' triumphal entry into Jerusalem. Give them the Bibles and suggest that they read the story from Mark 11:1–10 in groups of four. Encourage them to collaborate in the writing of the story and then present their stories to the rest of the class.

They might use interviews, on the scene reports, drawings, feature stories, advertising (commercials), etc.

32. Asking for Forgiveness

Introduction

This service recalls the betrayal of Judas and the denial of Peter. Both were close companions of Jesus and both chose to turn away from him, one from greed, the other from fear. It reminds children that no matter what his friends did, Jesus was willing to forgive them.

To Prepare

If possible, gather supplies for making small crosses: twigs and string, popsicle sticks and glue, paper and scissors, etc. On your prayer table place a sign with a cross on it that reads "Thank you for loving us, Jesus." Also place there a Bible (open to John 13:21–33,36–38) and a votive candle.

Leader	Jesus knew and loved his first followers, just as he knows and loves us today. We say that we believe in him and want to follow him, but we make mistakes. May Jesus forgive us as he forgave his apostles.
All	Lord Jesus Christ, son of the living God, have mercy on us.
Reader One	Jesus became very sad and his followers all noticed it. Finally he said to them, "I have to tell you something that troubles me very much. One of you is going to betray me this very night." *The Gospel of the Lord.*
All	Praise to you, Lord Jesus Christ.
Reader Two	Forgive us, Jesus, when we are rude or impatient with one another. Forgive us when we are selfish or disrespectful.
All	Lord Jesus Christ, son of the living God, have mercy on us.
Reader Three	Forgive us when we hurt the feelings of classmates or teachers, or when we disappoint our friends.
All	Lord Jesus Christ, son of the living God, have mercy on us.
Leader	Jesus, Judas betrayed you on the night of the Last Supper, and Peter denied that he ever knew you. And yet, you loved them. Thank you that you love us too.
	Pause for a moment of silent prayer.
Leader	During Holy Week, let us talk to Jesus often about our need for strength and courage to love and serve others in his name. We believe in you, Jesus; please help our unbelief.

All   Lord Jesus Christ, son of the living God, have mercy on us. Amen.

Lenten Action   Distribute the supplies you have gathered for making small crosses and show children how to put them together. Encourage them to keep these in a visible place at home as a reminder that Jesus loves them and always forgives them.

**Optional
Activity**   Review with children some of the ways they can say they are sorry when they have given in to weakness or sin. Following are some prayers you might want to share (and/or review) with them.

•O my God, I am heartily sorry for having offended you, and I detest all my sins because of your just punishments. I firmly resolve with the help of your grace to sin no more and to avoid the near occasions of sin. Amen.

•Dear God, I am your child and I love you very much. Sometimes I am not the best child I can be, and I am sorry for those times. Forgive me, please, and help me to try again to love and serve you and others. Amen.

•I confess to almighty God, and to you, my brothers and sisters, that I have sinned through my own fault, in my thoughts and in my words, in what I have done and in what I have failed to do; and I ask blessed Mary, ever virgin, all the angels and saints, and you, my brothers and sisters, to pray for me to the Lord, Our God.

33. Following Jesus

Introduction

This service focuses on the crucifixion of Jesus. You might want to pray it on or near Good Friday. It teaches children that what happened to Jesus did not end on Good Friday. Jesus continues to be "crucified" every time someone among us is treated poorly.

To Prepare

Place a cross or crucifix on your prayer table as well as a Bible (open to John 18:1–19:42) and a votive candle.

Leader	When Jesus was on trial, the people cried out, "Crucify him, crucify him." Every year we hear these words and wonder how those people could have been so cruel. Yet we have many opportunities to reach out to people who are suffering today. When we ignore their needs, we are ignoring Jesus in our midst.
All	Remind us today, Jesus, that what we do for others, we do for you.
Reader One	Pilate said to the leaders of the people, "Look at this man." He wanted them to see that Jesus had suffered enough. But they all cried out, "Crucify him, crucify him!" …In the end, Pilate handed him over to be crucified. *The Gospel of the Lord.*
All	Praise be to you, Lord Jesus Christ.
Reader Two	As you hung on the cross, Jesus, you prayed, "Father, forgive them." Please forgive us, too, for the times we forget that you are among us, for the times we forget to love and serve others.
All	Remind us today, Jesus, that what we do for others, we do for you.
Reader Two	Strengthen us to be your followers by standing up for what is right, for speaking out against what is wrong.
All	Remind us today, Jesus, that what we do for others, we do for you.
Leader	Let us now talk to Jesus, each in our own words, about our call to love and serve others in his name.
	Pause for a moment of silent prayer.
Leader	Jesus, you are our savior; you loved us and forgave us even from the cross. Thank you for these and all your gifts to us…

All   Amen.

Lenten Action   Solemnly take the cross from your prayer table and pass it from one child to the next as you pray: "Teach (child's name) how to follow you, Jesus." Children can answer, "Amen." Encourage children to say this prayer at home during Holy Week.

**Optional
Activity**   Invite the children in your class to pray the stations of the cross in church on or before Good Friday. Or plan a "Way of the Cross" in your teaching space. Mark the fourteen stops with a sign that describes what happened at each, and move with the children from one to the next, reflecting on how Jesus felt at each stop. If you are using a stations booklet, be sure to adapt it to the age level of those in your class.

34. Waiting for Easter

Introduction

This service encourages the children themselves to be proclaimers of the presence of Jesus, not just at Easter but all year through.

To Prepare

Place on your prayer table a Bible (open to Mark 16:15), a votive candle, paper and pencils for each participant, and a poster with these words printed on it: "Share the Good News!"

Leader

On Easter Sunday we will hear the words: "Alleluia, Alleluia!" This means "Praise God," but we use the word "Alleluia" because it is such a happy sound. Long after Easter Sunday is over, we can still pray with the words "Alleluia, Alleluia!" This is because Christians are so happy about the resurrection of Jesus that they want to keep on remembering it all year long.

Reader One

One of the ways we can keep the joy of the resurrection in our hearts and minds is to tell other people about it. We can spread the good news that Jesus is risen from the dead and is still with us in spirit. This is what Jesus asked his followers to do when he spoke to them after the resurrection. Let's listen to what he said.

Reader Two

A reading from the Gospel of Mark: After he had risen from the dead, Jesus showed himself to his followers while they were at supper. First he scolded them for not believing that he was alive. And then he said to them: "Go out to the whole world; spread the good news that I am alive to all creation."

Reader Three

After he had spoken to them, he was taken up to heaven; there at the right hand of God he took his place. His followers, doing as he asked, went out and spread the good news. *The Gospel of the Lord.*

All

Praise to you, Lord Jesus Christ.

Reader Four

We, too, are followers of Jesus, and so, we, too, should spread the Good News that Jesus is alive. One way we can do this is by remembering it ourselves. We can recall that Jesus is still with us and we can talk to Jesus in our hearts.

Leader   Another way is to show by our words and actions that we are followers of the risen Jesus. Remember the words of Jesus: "Spread the good news that I am alive to the whole world." Let us now join hands as we pray:

All   Jesus, we want to share the good news
that you are alive and among us through your Holy Spirit.
Teach us how to show others that we believe in you.
We're very happy that you are
risen and here with us now.
 Alleluia, Alleluia. Amen.

Lenten Action   Explain to children that one good way to proclaim the resurrection of Jesus is by making someone an Easter card. Distribute the paper and pencils. Older children can choose to whom they wish to write an Easter message and address their letters accordingly. Younger children might simply write a message to take home, for example: "Be happy, Jesus is with us always."

Encourage children to deliver their messages either by mail or in person.

35. Sharing Easter Joy

Introduction

Easter is the greatest feast of the church year since all of the events recorded in the gospels lead up to and point toward the resurrection. Jesus suffered, died, and was buried, but he was raised up on the third day. This is part and parcel of our Christian faith. This service then emphasizes our great call to follow Jesus and to share the joy of his resurrection. It encourages children to examine their lives and to reflect on daily ways to grow in faith. (Note that the opening prayer has been adapted from the *Te Deum*, an ancient prayer of the church.)

To Prepare

Place on your prayer table a large white candle and a Bible (open to Mark 16:2–7).

Leader   You, Christ, are the King of glory, eternal son of the Father. When you became man to set us free, you did not turn away from Mary's womb.

Reader One   You overcame the sting of death and opened the kingdom of heaven to all believers. You are seated at God's right hand in glory. We believe that you will come and be our judge.

Reader Two   Come, then, Jesus; sustain your people, bought with the price of your own blood, and bring us with your saints to everlasting glory.

All   Glory be to the Father, and to the Son, and to the Holy Spirit. As it was in the beginning, is now, and ever shall be, world without end. Amen.

Leader   The gospels tell us that Jesus was arrested, that he suffered and died on the cross, and that he was laid in a tomb. But they also tell us that Jesus was raised up by God. By his death and resurrection, he has set us free. Imagine how surprised his followers were on that first Easter Sunday when they went to the tomb.

Reader Three   A reading adapted from the Gospel of Mark:

Very early on the first day of the week they went to the tomb when the sun had risen…. And entering the tomb, they saw God's messenger sitting on the right side, dressed in a white robe; and they were amazed. "Do not be amazed," they were told; "you seek Jesus who was crucified. He has risen, he is not here; see the place where they laid him. But go, tell his disciples this good news. Jesus is risen." *The Gospel of the Lord.*

All   Praise to you, Lord Jesus Christ.

Leader   I invite you now to close your eyes and imagine that you are one of the people who have gone to the tomb on that early morning. What are you talking about as you go? What happens when you enter the tomb, expecting to find a body for anointing? What do you say to one another when you run out to find the disciples?

Tell Jesus now in your own words how you feel about the message from the angel: "He is not here; he is risen from the dead." Share with Jesus those times when your faith has not been strong, when you have failed to believe in his presence through your weakness and sin. Ask for his forgiveness now.

Allow two to three minutes for silent prayer.

Leader   Jesus, though your messenger asked us to spread the good news of your resurrection, we often forget to tell it. Teach us how to love you and follow you as we should. Teach us how to give witness to you every day of our lives. We ask these things…

All   In the name of the Father, and of the Son, and of the Holy Spirit. Amen.

Lenten Action   Invite the children to role-play the resurrection scene described in the reading from the Gospel of Mark. Or, better yet, invite them to role-play this scene in a contemporary setting. Tell them to include what they would say to the disciples, once they found them. Afterward spend some time discussing these questions:

- What do you say to people today about the resurrection?
- Do you announce the good news in any way in your daily life?
- How might you begin to do this?

36. Receiving the Holy Spirit

Introduction

This service emphasizes the presence of Jesus through his Holy Spirit. It can be used on or near Pentecost, but is also appropriate for year-round use. Children studying the sacraments, particularly confirmation, might benefit from this emphasis on the gift of the Holy Spirit.

To Prepare

Beforehand, make small verse cards for each child on which are printed the words: "Come, Holy Spirit." Place these in a container on your prayer table as well as a Bible (open to John 14:23–27) and a votive candle.

Leader	The grace of our Lord Jesus Christ, the love of God, and the fellowship of the Holy Spirit be with you all.
All	And also with you.
Leader	On the night before he died, Jesus promised his followers that he would give them wonderful gifts, especially the gift of the Holy Spirit. Listen to the words he used.
Reader One	A reading from the Gospel of John: If you love me, Jesus said, you will keep my word, and my Father will love you, and we shall come to you and make our home with you. Those who do not love me do not keep my word…
Reader Two	I have said these things to you while I am still with you, but the Holy Spirit, the one whom the Father will send to you in my name, will teach you everything and remind you of all that I have said. *The Gospel of the Lord.*
All	Praise to you, Lord Jesus Christ.
Leader	Let us now ask the Holy Spirit to be with us in a special way and to remind us of all that Jesus has taught us. Holy Spirit, you are our companion and friend…
All	Come, Holy Spirit.
Leader	You are our teacher and helper…
All	Come, Holy Spirit.
Leader	You are our guide and comforter…

All	Come, Holy Spirit.
Leader	Jesus has offered us the gift of the Holy Spirit. It is through the presence of the Spirit that he is with us. Often throughout the day we can pray by saying, "Come, Holy Spirit."
All	Come, Holy Spirit, and fill us with love and forgiveness. Come with your grace and heavenly aid to fill the hearts that God has made. Come, Holy Spirit. Amen.
Pentecost Action	Call each child by name and when each comes forward, present him or her with a verse card while saying: "(Child's name), receive this card and remember that the Spirit of Jesus is always with you." Invite the children to decorate their cards and to place them in their rooms at home as a prayer reminder.

37. Living in the Spirit

Introduction

This Pentecost service focuses on the presence of the Holy Spirit. Remind children before the service that in order to stay among us, Jesus sent us his Spirit. Allow sufficient time for questions and/or discussion about what this means.

To Prepare

On your prayer table place a Bible (open to Acts 2:1–4), a votive candle, and precut "tongues of fire" (flames), one for each participant. On a large piece of posterboard, write the words "We are filled with the Holy Spirit," and place this, too, on or near the table.

Leader	Glory be to the Father, and to the Son, and to the Holy Spirit...
All	As it was in the beginning, is now, and ever shall be, world without end. Amen.
Leader	After his resurrection, Jesus was "taken up to heaven." At his request, his followers were to wait together in prayer for a sign from him. This sign would assure them that Jesus would be with them always. They probably had no clear idea about what to expect or when to expect it. This is how God's Word, the Bible, describes the sign that Jesus sent.
Reader One	A reading from the Acts of the Apostles: All the believers were gathered together in one place. Suddenly there was a noise from the sky that sounded like a strong wind blowing, and it filled the whole house where they were sitting.
Reader Two	Then they saw what looked like tongues of fire that spread out and touched each person there. They were all filled with the Holy Spirit and began to talk in other languages as the Spirit taught them to speak. *The Word of the Lord.*
All	Thanks be to God.
Leader	The sign sent by Jesus was the Holy Spirit, the Spirit of Jesus himself! Jesus would now be with his followers, not in his earthly form, but through the Holy Spirit.
Reader Three	The first followers immediately felt the effects of the Holy Spirit. And today followers of Jesus, like us, continue to feel the presence of the Holy Spirit.

Reader Four   According to the promise of Jesus, the Holy Spirit is among us whenever we gather in the name of Jesus. We don't see the Holy Spirit, but we can believe in the promise of Jesus; we can believe that Jesus is with us.

Leader   Let us now join hands and pray: Glory be to the Father, and to the Son, and to the Holy Spirit…

All   As it was in the beginning, is now, and ever shall be, world without end. Amen.

Pentecost Action   Give each child one of the cut-out flames and ask them to place their names on it and to decorate it. When all are decorated, invite children to attach them to the poster on your prayer table. Decide together where you will keep your "Spirit" poster. Or, ask the children if they would like to take turns displaying the poster in their homes.

38. Walking with the Spirit

Introduction

Pentecost is a special occasion to share with children the good news that God offers us unconditional love and forgiveness through the presence of the Holy Spirit. Jesus, not wanting to leave us orphans, sent the Spirit to remind us of all that he said, did, and taught. The Holy Spirit dwells in the church and in us, assuring us that God is always offering love, acceptance, and forgiveness.

To Prepare

Have available blank, precut pieces of cardboard (2" x 6"), and pencils or markers for the activity. On your prayer table place a Bible (open to John 15:16–20 or John 21:19–23), a votive candle, and a poster that reads: "Come, Holy Spirit."

Leader	I invite you to say this prayer with me by repeating each line after me: Come, Holy Spirit, creator blest,
All	Come, Holy Spirit, creator blest,
Leader	and in our hearts take up your rest.
All	and in our hearts take up your rest.
Leader	Come with your grace and heavenly aid,
All	Come with your grace and heavenly aid,
Leader	and fill the hearts that you have made.
All	and fill the hearts that you have made.
Leader	The church celebrates the feast of Pentecost fifty days after Easter. During the Easter season we focus on the resurrection of Jesus and his appearances to his followers after he was raised up. On Pentecost, we celebrate the presence of Jesus through the Holy Spirit. At the Last Supper, Jesus promised his followers that he would send them the Holy Spirit, which is his own spirit, as a way of staying with them.
Reader One	Jesus said to his followers: "I will ask the Father and he will give you another helper to be with you always. This helper is the Spirit of Truth whom the world will not recognize, but you will recognize the Spirit,

because it will be within you.
See, I will not leave you orphaned;
I will come back to you."

Leader   After he had been raised from the dead, Jesus appeared to his followers and gave them the power to forgive sins, but he made it clear that they could only do this because of their faith in the Holy Spirit. Jesus was giving them the right to represent him and to offer his gift of forgiveness to people, but they could only do this if they lived in the presence of the Holy Spirit.

Reader Two   Jesus came and stood before his followers and said:
"Peace be with you."
He showed them the wound marks on his hands and side,
and they knew then that it was he.
"Peace be with you," he said again.
Then he breathed on them and said:
"Receive the Holy Spirit.
The sins you forgive in my name shall be forgiven."
The Gospel of the Lord.

All   Praise to you, Lord Jesus Christ.

Leader   Let us now ask the Holy Spirit to guide us always. Please respond: Holy Spirit, come fill our hearts.

Reader Three   That we might believe in the promise of Jesus that he has given us the Holy Spirit to be with us always…

All   Holy Spirit, come fill our hearts.

Reader Four   That we might be truly sorry for the times we have not lived in the presence of Jesus and his Spirit…

All   Holy Spirit, come fill our hearts.

Leader   I invite you now to close your eyes and picture yourself walking into the reconciliation room. Sitting there is not the priest, but Jesus himself! You go and sit beside him. He welcomes you and explains to you that later when you speak to the priest in confession, you will be also speaking to him. He has given the priest the permission to forgive you in his name.

Tell Jesus now whatever is in your heart. Talk to him about whatever it is that troubles you.

Allow time for quiet prayer.